JOB SATISFACTION IMPROVEMENT

The Four Corners Framework Method for Better Job Happiness

Murray E. L. Reeves

ISBN-13: 9798726682228

Cover design by: Art Painter
Library of Congress Control Number: 2018675309
Printed in the United States of America

CONTENTS

Title Page

Copyright

Foreword   1

Chapter 1: Introduction   6

Chapter 2: Understanding Job Satisfaction and Engagement   13

Chapter 3: The Four Corners Framework   23

Chapter 4: The Four Corners Framework Self-Assessment   31
Process

Chapter 5: Self-Assessment Interpretation and Four Corners   37
Insight

Chapter 6: Transition Plans   51

Chapter 7: Closing the Bad State-Good State Gaps   57

Chapter 8: Thoughts on Attributes   65

Chapter 9: Summary   93

Afterword   97

FOREWORD

"True happiness is to enjoy the present, without anxious dependence upon the future, not to amuse ourselves with either hopes or fears but to rest satisfied with what we have, which is sufficient, for he that is so wants nothing. The greatest blessings of mankind are within us and within our reach. A wise man is content with his lot, whatever it may be, without wishing for what he has not."

Lucius Annaeus Seneca

We are taught early in our life to value and admire ambition, achievement, and advancement. You should be "committed to your job, and the success of your organization" we are instructed. At first read of the quote above, Seneca seems to be proposing that to be happy one must dispense with all of this. What Seneca is really advocating, however, is the importance of maintaining perspective. Not to dispense with achievement and advancement, but to exalt in the moment-to-moment experience of it. To recognize the value of each moment of life experience, whether reaching for success or struggling with adversity, is the essence of his message.

How difficult is it to think this way about our work? Apparently quite difficult. Published workplace surveys point to a disturbing percentage of people unhappy in their jobs. These surveys show a remarkable consistency over years of data collection - different generations and different economic conditions show similar levels of unsatisfied workers. At the same time, paradoxically, there is virtual unanimity in studies for employers that profess the powerful and positive effects on productivity and employee retention that come from improved job satisfaction. We want to be satisfied. Our employers should want us to be satisfied. Where is the disconnect?

Our first inclination when we are unhappy at a job is to "throw it away" - get rid of it and find a better new one, like we do with so much else in our modern lives. We get plenty of reinforcement for this thinking as well. Expressing dissatisfaction and frustration with our job is commonly met with advice of "You should quit." and "You deserve better!" from friends and family. Our second inclination is to look to our organization for the solution. "Why can't my company/manager/pay/assignments be better? Then I'd be happier."

For some people a change of job may be the right path. But for many of us our life circumstances may not make it that simple to quit and look for something different that is only *hopefully* better.

When I look at publications professing help and advice for working people unsatisfied with their jobs, the advice that is offered is largely on how to find your dream job. Very little is written in depth about how to improve your current circumstances. These articles and books are predominantly written by psychologists, staffing specialists, or business consultants. Rarely are they from deeply experienced managers - people who have spent their careers on the front lines of the environment you work in.

I've been in the work world for over 36 years. My first role as a manager was back in 1989. Since then, I've worked and managed in a wide variety of circumstances: in small teams and big teams, in high growth business cycles and business shutdowns. I've managed remote resources and international resources. I've encountered big successes and big crises. I've worked for many managers and have managed managers. I've completed numerous courses and read much on team building, people management and people interaction. This in total has given me thousands of hours of broad and practical "street-level" education on what drives job satisfaction.

This course is for those people who want to take control and improve their own job satisfaction - both for their current employment and for future jobs. It is for people striving to gain a better appreciation for what they have, and better insight into what, in fact, they really need. I offer this process for job satisfaction improvement in the hopes that it can help people achieve it.

The Coronavirus Pandemic

The coronavirus pandemic emerged as I was completing this book. I felt I should add a note acknowledging this, and the potential effect it might have on the book content.

The short-term effect of the pandemic on workers has ranged widely, from having workplaces temporarily shut down to shifting employees to work-from-home for social distancing. In the longer term I believe that there will be a significant change in jobs that are compatible with work-from-home.

The feasibility of conducting work from home for many office jobs has systematically increased for decades. There has been a constant improvement in productivity and communications tools to enable this, such as cell phones, internet video meeting applications, and chat applications. These have all made the arrangement quite viable. Employers have only dabbled in exploring this. Some offered modest flexibility, like occasional work-from-home days. Others were less flexible. The job satisfaction studies I've read point to work hour and location flexibility as significant factors in improving job satisfaction.

So why wasn't work-from-home been incorporated more liberally into the working world? I believe the main factor is that, as this book points out, managers generally are poorly trained in the skills of people management. They therefore feel much more comfortable when they can "see" their employees working to keep tabs on productivity. They are also able to drop by an employee's workstation whenever a whim crosses their mind about needing a status update on an assignment, or a new assignment comes to mind.

The pandemic forced a large experiment onto many organizations, and consequently managers. They were dropped in the deep end of remote resource management, and also had to participate themselves. Simultaneously organizations learned that their businesses could function adequately without having employees at their desks. Management leadership looking around at the empty office now see an opportunity - cost savings associated with expensive office space. In addition, a workplace that effectively incorporated work-from-home is no longer limited to the local resources to fill job openings. They now can consider candidates from far and wide, and without the expense of employee relocation.

There is a catch, however. Studies have shown that workers fall into two broad categories: Some people much prefer working from home, some not. Productivity follows preference, so the workplaces still need to sort out how best to accommodate both situations.

Regarding job satisfaction, this should be a good thing overall. The option of working from home means more flexibility in dealing with issues of Environment, Relationships, and Compensation, as you will see in the book. The main challenge will be in the change associated with the most dominant attribute in job satisfaction - Manager relationship. Learning how to communicate effectively, develop trust, and work productively through only electronic communications will be a new level of challenge to both employees and managers.

CHAPTER 1: INTRODUCTION

"Pleasure in the job puts perfection in the work."
Aristotle

When someone asks you "How satisfied are you with your job?" I'm sure you have some kind of a response at hand. It may not be a detailed one, and maybe it depends on the type of day you just had. At the simplest level you recognize that you enjoy your work, you tolerate it, or you hate it.

You may be surprised to hear that lots of people on our planet are not that happy with their job or work environment. I first looked at a worldwide analysis done by Aon, "2017 Trends in Global Employee Engagement", to quantify this. In summary it concludes that **one third (33%) of employees worldwide are "not engaged at work"**. This means that they:

Do not say positive things about their organization and do not act as advocates

Do not intend to stay at their organization for a long time, and

Are not motivated to strive to give their best efforts to help the organization succeed

Another large U.S. study that I reviewed, Gallup's comprehensive

2017 "State of the American Workplace", reports that:

> "The American workforce has more than 100 million full-time employees. One-third of those employees are what Gallup calls "engaged at work". They love their jobs and make their organization and America better every day. At the other end, 16% of employees are actively disengaged—they are miserable in the workplace and destroy what the most engaged employees build. The remaining 51% of employees are not engaged—they're just there."

In 2020 Gallup wrote a paper on 2019 results titled **"4 Factors Driving Record-High Employee Engagement in U.S."**. In it they stated:

> "Gallup found that in 2019, the percentage of "engaged" workers in the U.S. -- those who are highly involved in, enthusiastic about and committed to their work and workplace -- reached 35%. This is a new high since Gallup began tracking the metric in 2000. The percentage of workers who are "actively disengaged" -- those who have miserable work experiences and spread their unhappiness to their colleagues -- tied its lowest level (13%), consistent with the 2018 finding."

A new high of 35% engaged since Gallup started this tracking in 2006 still left 52% "not engaged", and 13% "actively disengaged". This still leaves the majority of the U.S. workforce indifferent to, or even hating their job.

Gallup Poll: 2019 The American Workplace

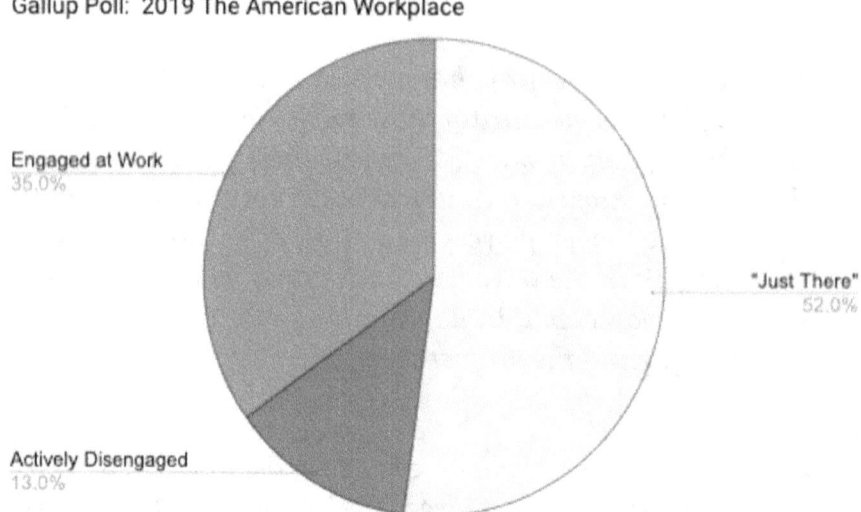

Engaged at Work
35.0%

"Just There"
52.0%

Actively Disengaged
13.0%

Incredible. This means 13% plus 52% - a total of 65% of employees - are either sleepwalking through their job or hate it so much that they use their time to *undermine* their employer and work environment! With only one-third of employees *engaged* at work this means that between you, your coworker on the left and the one on the right, statistically only one of you is that rare individual that actually *likes* coming to work!

Did you know that if you work full time from your 20's to your 60's you will spend somewhere between *70,000* and *100,000* hours at work? Typically, *over 40% of your waking life* is spent working! You sacrifice time with family, friends, hobbies and other self-interests to work. You may even sacrifice your health. Shouldn't something be done to make this time spent enjoyable and happy?

It turns out that job satisfaction is important not just to you but to your employer as well. Studies show with remarkable consistency that the more a person is satisfied with their work:

    - The more productive they are

- The less likely they are to change to another job or company

- The more likely they are to experience better emotional health

If you work for a large organization, or just a particularly good one, structured effort to improve your job satisfaction might be found in **Employee SAT**isfaction (**ESAT**) programs. ESAT is the broad term used for evaluation and continuous improvement of a company's overall state of employee satisfaction. These include employee surveys, subsequent analysis, presentations and discussion of survey results and improvement plans with employees. An ESAT program is a genuine attempt by your company to identify the issues diminishing employee job satisfaction, and effort to figure out how to address them.

The limitation with ESAT programs is that they predominantly identify and act on collective issues - those that affect a broad group of employees. ESAT will identify problems such as poor company direction and general communication, insufficient training, or inefficient and frustrating business processes. These are worthwhile things to address but, unless your issues are the same as the average employee in the survey, nothing significant is changing for you. And this assumes that your workplace even has an ESAT initiative. Only a small percentage of organizations are big enough, or motivated enough, to have formal ESAT programs and initiatives.

So where does that leave you if you are experiencing low workplace satisfaction? Typically, employees are encouraged to go to their manager, or Human Resources (HR) with their concerns and problems and try to work out improvement that way.

Let us consider the route of approaching managers first. My observation has been that excellent managers are about as common as excellent teachers. Think back through all of your schooling. How many *great* teachers did you encounter? Not just good or capable teachers, but ones that could get you excited about a subject that otherwise might have been boring; ones that could really relate to, communicate with, and motivate students, and you in particular. Typically, people can only count one or two in the dozens of teachers they've had. Many of the teachers knew their teaching subject well, conveyed it in a competent way, and cared that they were getting through to students. Some were, bluntly, just not that good.

Managers are similar. Most have been promoted to the role because they know the subject of their job well. They've demonstrated initiative and ambition, and leadership - or at least leadership potential. Unfortunately, very few managers get real training on the soft skills needed to manage the difficult problem of what to do with unhappy and unmotivated employees. Natural aptitude in these skills is no better than third or fourth on the hierarchy of selection criteria for promotion to manager (the first three being: technical competence, "fit" with the promoting manager, and demonstration of initiative or leadership). In the vast majority of cases, managers get educated on soft skills from the "streets" - this means experiencing what works and doesn't work from their own managers, as well as from observing and interacting in the workplace.

It is also common that managers - especially first level managers - are very heavily tasked with projects, daily activities, administrative work and periodic deliverables. The sum of all this is that managers have little time - and sometimes little patience - to try to fit their employees job satisfaction into a tightly packed workload. Try talking to your manager about how you are not feeling that motivated at work when she/he has major deadlines looming. It's liable to be a short, distracted conversation. This is not to say that managers can't be helpful or conscientious in trying to improve your workplace satisfaction. Many take this very seriously. It's a question of understanding and effectiveness.

What about the idea of going to your HR representative with your job satisfaction concern? Decades ago, an HR representative was someone you might have gone to for a heart-to-heart about how you were feeling about your job, or even non-work issues. Now HR will defer this back to managers or send you to Employee Assistance Plan (EAP) counselling, if this is a benefit your company offers. Typically, an HR Representative has a large number of employees and managers that they are responsible for. This limits the time they have available for even attempting to perform counselling activities themselves, even if they were allowed to.

Unfortunately, if you are not as satisfied or engaged at work you are most likely alone in figuring out what you can do about it. It really comes down to that old saying: "If you want something done right, you have to do it yourself." But frankly, if you don't take ownership of *your own job satisfaction*, why should those around you care to do it for you?

Improving your own job satisfaction is not easy. Too often our first thought though is to leave the job and find a better one. That may not be possible, easy, or even be advisable. If your job meets your basic needs - allows you to pay your bills, provides you with benefits, gives you seniority and employment security - leaving it may be risky and costly, without any guarantee that the next job will solve your problems. It may even introduce new ones! Our reasons for commitment to a job can be sufficient for us to stay with a job even if we are unhappy in it.

If you've decided that looking for a new job is not an acceptable option, you've likely landed on one of two other courses of action. You may be thinking that the only way to survive at your job is to stop complaining and grind through each day - at the risk of *losing your mind*. Or maybe you thought you need to alleviate frustration by changing your behavior to accommodate co-workers and management - "suck up", in other words - at the cost of *selling your soul*.

The approach I'm presenting is about a third way. It is about identifying the specific problems constraining your satisfaction and exploring ways to affect positive, constructive, change both in your environment and in your personal approach to your job. Importantly, it is also how to implement these changes yourself. Learning the skill of how to clarify *your* satisfaction needs and get them in place through *your own* initiative will not only make you happier and more successful in your current job, but you will become better at achieving this in *any future job*. The goal is not just *surviving* but *thriving* at work!

The *Four Corners Framework* is a process designed to empower you to take control of your own job satisfaction. Professional, white collar, blue collar, government, contractor, public or private sector, for-profit or not-for-profit organization employees - all can make use of this approach. The skills you need are basic. If you can write in a journal, and follow a plan, you're there (by the way, get yourself a journal and a pen!!). The hardest parts of this process are to be honest with yourself, be open to new ideas and approaches, and be courageous enough to take control of your circumstances instead of being a victim of them!

CHAPTER 2: UNDERSTANDING JOB SATISFACTION AND ENGAGEMENT

"Very little is needed to make a happy life. It is within yourself, in your way of thinking."

Marcus Aurelius

What Is "Satisfaction"?

This question sounds somewhat absurd. It's almost like asking someone if they know what "warm" and "cold" is. If you were asked to picture someone who is satisfied, I'm sure that you would find that easy. But if you were asked how to *make* a person satisfied you might have lots of questions.

There are many companies and individuals that make their living studying how to make the workplace more productive and efficient. How workers feel about their job and work environment emerges as a major factor in these studies. Typical workplace analysis studies use *"Satisfaction"* and *"Engagement"* as the primary terms for how employees feel about their work and work environment. The management consulting company *Decision-Wise* defines these terms this way:

"**Satisfaction** is based on a **transactional relationship.** It's an implied (or explicit) contract—a this-for-that exchange. In a satisfaction-oriented environment, I work because I receive adequate compensation. When I don't feel that compensation is adequate, my commitment to the job or the organization wanes. My effort will be commensurate with what I receive."

"**Engagement**, on the other hand, involves **discretionary effort.** The term "discretionary" implies that there is additional effort available on the part of the employee that he or she can CHOOSE to apply if so motivated. However, the choice to apply this effort is something not stated in the satisfaction contract—it's up to the employee. In essence, satisfaction is a feeling of **satiation**, whereas engagement is a feeling of **activation.**"

In other words, if you're **satisfied** at work you feel that essentially you can add up all the positives (the fun tasks, compensation, environment, opportunities, etc.) and subtract the negatives (the aggravations, conflicts, sacrifices and frustrations) and it balances out. You're not taking advantage of your employer and your employer is not taking advantage of you. It follows that if you're **engaged** at work you're getting all you need out of work and more. You feel like you can throw extra into work - extra hours, extra effort, more positivity. Work is not just an obligation or a source of money, it's fun and rewarding - even an investment.

Organizations regularly use surveys to assess the satisfaction level of their workforce. These surveys probe what factors employees feel are important about their job and work environment. Then they ask the employees to measure or rank how satisfied they are with each aspect polled in the survey. These surveys can include numerous categories, dozens of questions in each category, and various levels for the employee to rank their response to each job factor, or "attribute". For example, there may be an attribute category on managers, with a question and assessment similar to:

	Disagree		Not Sure		Agree
My manager does a good job of communicating work priorities to me in a timely fashion.	1	2	3	4	5

These question responses can then be analyzed to form a con-clusion about the attitudes employees have towards an attrib-ute category. In the case of the example above, analysis of the "Manager" question set may indicate that employees are or not satisfied with aspects of the way they are managed. This result can then be presented by the organization's leaders to employees with a plan to make appropriate improvements.

Decades of these types of studies have distilled job attributes and the categories they form into familiar, common lists. For ex-ample: quality of management, compensation, advancement op-portunities, company culture, etc. This process has evolved to provide organizations with feedback in a form that they can use to act on to improve their overall employee satisfaction.

Any given individual taking the survey might find that the con-cerns about their job line up well to the questions a survey is asking. There is a good chance, however, that a person's spe-cific issues get diluted in the analysis, or maybe are missed al-together. While there is usually opportunity in the surveys for the employee to provide some comments regarding their specific concerns, the objective of these surveys is to identify the broader organization results. A more complete and personal way to look at job satisfaction is for a worker to analyze this from the bottom up - to first understand what fundamentally drives the individ-ual's satisfaction, and then assess how well these drivers are met.

To start constructing this process we first need to dig deeper to develop a clear understanding of what "satisfaction" fundamentally means, not at an organization's level but at a personal level. To launch this we can take a look at the definition of the word "satisfaction":

sat·is·fac·tion

/ˌsadəsˈfakSH(ə)n/ *noun*

Fulfillment of one's **needs**, **expectations**, or **wishes**, or the pleasure derived from this.

This begs us to excavate another level so that we can understand the individual definitions of **Needs**, **Expectations**, and **Wishes**. Once again, from the dictionary:

need

/nēd/ *Verb*

Require (something) because it is essential or very important.

ex·pec·ta·tion

/ˌekspekˈtāSH(ə)n/ *noun*

A strong belief that something will happen or be the case in the future.

wish

/wiSH/ *Verb*

Feel or express a strong desire or hope for something that is not easily attainable; want something that cannot or probably will not happen.

We can combine these three contributors into a statement that provides an explicit understanding of the meaning of Satisfaction:

Satisfaction is the fulfillment of those things that we deem are essential, those things that we believe strongly that we deserve, and those things that we desire or hope for.

Satisfaction is therefore a mix of having what we can't do without, what we deserve, and what hard work, luck or providence provides us. What a recipe! No wonder we struggle to be satisfied when we expect it to just "arrive" at our doorstep without a conscious process to create it!

It is clear that defining a given job attribute as a *need*, an *expectation* or a *wish* can vary from person to person. This definition can also change over time and circumstances. If you or your family is experiencing starvation or homelessness, any job that provides the income to meet these needs will bring satisfaction. If you've invested thousands of dollars and years of education towards qualifications, however, your satisfaction in a job will be tied to strong expectations of short-term success and advancement.

Some attributes of our work are much harder to categorize. Salary - or compensation - is a good example. At what point does your level of compensation change from a need to an expectation, or from an expectation to a wish? And how do we compare an "expected" compensation to, say, your relationship with your manager?

Making these distinctions is critically important to job satisfaction assessment. A general employee survey and company action plan *cannot* dig deep enough or be specific enough about what workplace attributes *you* value, how *you* value them as a need, expectation or wish. A better solution is to approach this from the individual's perspective. A logical, simple, framework is needed to help us define this process.

Understanding What Motivates Us

To get insight into what fulfills our needs, expectations, and wishes we can turn to Abraham Maslow, an American psychologist from the mid-1900's.

Maslow was fascinated about what drove human motivation - the desire to take action. He published a seminal paper in 1943 entitled "A Theory of Human Motivation" in the journal *Psychological Review* that defined the "needs" that drive us

American Psychologist Abraham Maslow, 1908–1970

to act, and how they were organized. An important part of the theory was the hierarchy concept, depicted in the "Hierarchy of Needs Pyramid":

Maslow's Hierarchy of Needs Pyramid

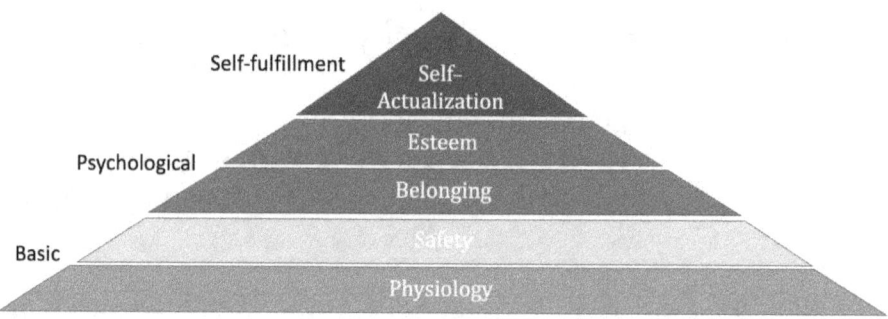

The pyramid lists the five fundamental needs. The hierarchical structure of the needs comes from the idea that before one pursued a higher need, the lower need was a priority to be fulfilled. For instance, before one could pursue Safety, one needed to fulfill Physiology - food and shelter - needs. Maslow also grouped needs as "Basic" (Physiology and Safety), "Psychological" (Belonging and Esteem), and "Self-fulfillment" (Self-actualization). The definitions of each of the five needs are as follows:

> *Physiology:* Basic biological needs for survival, such as air, water, food, and shelter

Safety: Basic needs to provide avoidance of physical or emotional danger

Belonging: Need for positive relationships and interpersonal interactions to provide companionship, affection

Esteem: Need for reputation or prestige, recognition, attention, importance, and appreciation

Self-Actualization: Need for personal fulfillment

Over the decades since its publication much research and data collection did follow. Academic theory on motivation has evolved, with the main feedback on Maslow's theory being different opinions on the rigidity of the hierarchy. Maslow's theory remains popular, however, even more than seventy seven years after its publication. Uriel Abulof (Abulof, Uriel (2017-12-01). "Introduction: Why We Need Maslow in the Twenty-First Century". *Society.* **54** (6): 508) explains this as follows:

> *"The continued resonance of Maslow's theory in popular imagination, however unscientific it may seem, is possibly the single most telling evidence of its significance: it explains human nature as something that most humans immediately recognize in themselves and others."*

Maslow's theory can be described as a "model" of how motivation is formed out of the five needs. What a model attempts to do is to describe the behavior of the "output" of a system by how it is affected by the "inputs":

Determining what inputs to include, how each drives the outcome, and how they interact is the challenge of creating a model. Models are very common in our world. They can involve extraordinarily complex physics, like climate change models. They can also be simpler, like how a diet affects your weight.

Predicting human motivation behavior is of course extraordinarily difficult. Humans are very complex systems. Identifying the important inputs, and how these inputs affect behavior is very challenging, and it is further complicated by our uniqueness as individuals - the variation in response to these inputs from person to person. Maslow's genius was to identify a simple list of five inputs and how they are organized such that virtually everyone can look at them as familiar and relevant. While we can only infer motivation level from this for people in general, someone using this model for themselves - with self-awareness as to how they are specifically influenced by the five inputs - might find excellent results.

Applying Maslow's Theory To Job Satisfaction

Maslow's theory applies to the full scope of our life, not just our job. As such we cannot expect our job to completely fulfill the Five Needs. We can and should expect our job to contribute to the

Needs, and as such Maslow's theory gives us a great starting point to structure our job satisfaction improvement plan from.

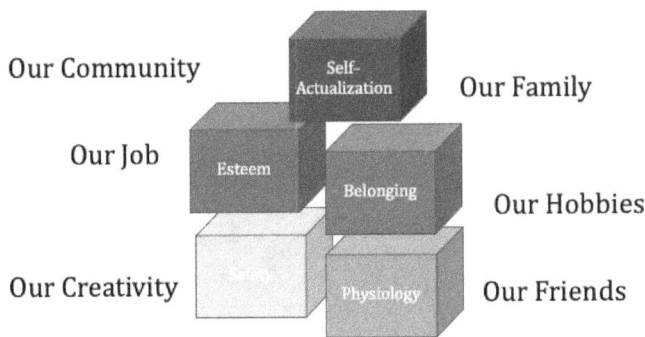

Our motivation in the specific area of our job is the desire to pursue actions that improve our job *Satisfaction*, and beyond that to achieving *Engagement*.

The drive behind these actions becomes the job attributes we value, which in turn comes from how these attributes map into Maslow's five fundamental needs.

Through careful assessment we can decide whether any attribute of our job constitutes a *need* or not. As we defined earlier, we must be clear that any attribute we consider a *need* is *"essential, or very important"*. These are attributes that contribute to our physiological and safety needs, in Maslow's model. But an attribute that is non-essential, or not currently attained, may still be important to us and our feeling of job satisfaction. These may fall into the category of *expectations* - those things that we believe will happen in the future, like a strong possibility of a raise or promotion. Without these *expectations* we might feel the job is a "dead end" even though it meets all our current *needs*. Likewise, with *wishes* that are less certain again. These categories for attributes allow us to sort the present from the future. Does our job currently provide a viable path to future needs? In Maslow's terms, we might be in a place in life and career where we see these *expectations* and *wishes* creating a path to Maslow's higher needs of Esteem and Self-Actualization.

CHAPTER 3: THE FOUR CORNERS FRAMEWORK

"The human being needs a framework of values, a philosophy of life, a religion or religion-surrogate to live by and understand by, in about the same sense that he needs sunlight, calcium or love."

Abraham Maslow

The Basic Idea

When I talk to people who are unsatisfied with their job and ask them why they are unhappy I commonly get the "stone-in-the-shoe" explanation - it's the result of a single predominant pain they are experiencing. "I don't like my manager", or "I'm not paid enough", or "I'm not appreciated" are typical examples. The pain this "stone" inflicts is obviously serious enough that it leads to tunnel-vision focus on this problem. Even worse, this is commonly accompanied by a sense that there are really no viable options for resolving it. Anything good about the job is completely overshadowed by this one, unsolvable problem. The only available resolution is to work somewhere else - a different department, or a different organization.

For something as important as a person's livelihood or career, avoiding rash decisions is really important. Enduring the problem for even another day may seem unbearable but making a hasty move under this pressure can risk trading one problem for another, or for many others. Sober second thought is even more obviously required for those who are unsatisfied at their job or satisfied but want to be more engaged. To do this we need to see clearly and completely the problem or problems with our job *alongside the positives*.

An ideal process points us to solutions instead of just problems, including how to stay at your job and resolve that "stone-in-the-shoe" issue. My career advice to people has been to run towards the job you want, rather than away from the job you don't. In this way the focus is on the solutions to achieve your needs, expectations and wishes rather than how to eliminate your frustrations. How many people know with completeness what they want in a job? How many people have even given this serious thought? Without this self-awareness one would expect a difficult time avoiding that one dominant problem and achieving real job satisfaction and engagement.

The process that I will lay out before you requires you to drive it. No lengthy company surveys, no ESAT programs. Instead of treating your job satisfaction like a restaurant goer where you are offered a menu, you will learn how to invade the kitchen and customize your order to your desire.

The Four Corners Framework

To assess a job, we commonly make a list of the things we like about it, and the things we don't, and then compare the results. I've found it challenging to do this in an unbiased way. My like-unlike list tends to grow longer on the side that I was leaning to before I started the list! I can also give greater importance to the items on my favored side to lean the outcome to my emotional preference. I'm sure I'm not the only one who does this. A good self-assessment process needs to be built in a way that allows our feelings to be included, but also pushes us to focus on the important things that will lead us to longer term satisfaction. Out of this process should emerge an increased self-awareness that we can use not only for our current job and organization, but all future ones as well.

The Four Corners Framework is a job satisfaction model. You will recall that we discussed what the purpose of a model is earlier - to help us understand the way a system works. The Four Corners Framework model identifies four fundamental categories of job attributes as inputs and how these categories connect to Maslow's needs.

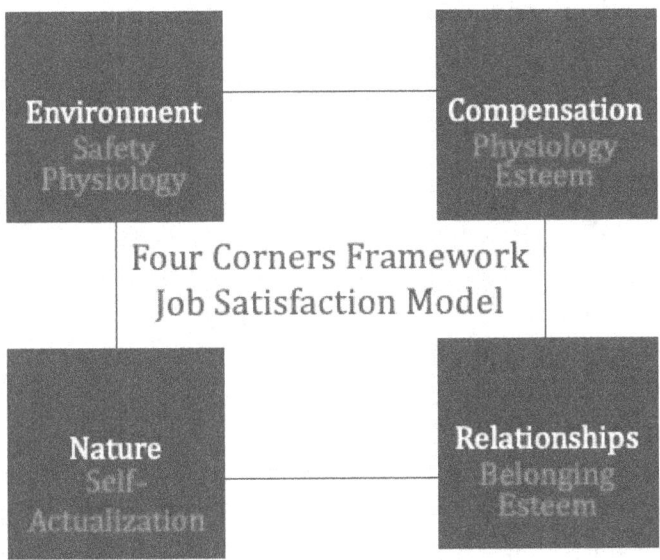

Each corner is built from a set of job attributes. Assessing these attributes individually will of course confirm the specific pain points we are aware of and experience at our job, but by combining them into the Four Corners themes it can also give us insight into fundamental needs met and not met that we are overlooking. This in turn helps us understand the likely output of our "system" - us - as we respond to the inputs. With a clearer understanding of how the system works, we can see how to improve it.

Before we dive deeper into the details let's look at a couple of conceptual examples. For the first let's say you are having a significant problem with how your manager is treating you at work.

This is obviously something that needs to be resolved. Looking beyond this for the moment, however, the rest of your work *Relationships* are good, you are happy with the *Environment*, your *Compensation* is excellent, and the *Nature* of your work - what you do - is enjoyable and stimulating. By looking at the broader picture it's apparent that the job meets all your needs, with the exception of the manager. This then warrants considerable effort (and maybe some creativity) to be put forth to improve the relationship with your manager. The "signal" here is that you have a job very well suited to your needs. The "noise" is the manager relationship overwhelming the positives.

A second example: You find yourself persistently tired and grumpy at work. You regularly think "They don't pay me enough to go through this aggravation - I need a raise!!" When you think about your *Compensation* at calmer times you have to admit you're actually well paid. You're managed well, work in a great team (*Relationships*), have exciting projects and can't imagine getting the opportunities and independence in another company (*Nature*). Upon reflection you realize that your terrible commute is ruining everything. You get up way too early so you're persistently tired, but if you go to bed early you miss important family time. The tedious traffic and unpredictability of commute time is incredibly aggravating. You realize that your work *Environment* - location - is more important than previously thought. With this knowledge in hand and the esteem you have at work, it turns out that when you discuss this with your manager, she is happy to authorize some flexibility in your work schedule - shifted hours to avoid most congested commute times, and work from home on bad weather days.

In the first example the manager problem falls under the *Relationships Cornerstone.* This relates to the Maslow needs of Esteem and Belonging. In the second example the commuting problem falls under the *Environment Cornerstone*. This relates to the Maslow need of Safety and Physiology, specifically the need for appropriate rest.

Let us now look into the detailed definitions of the *Four Corners* and the attributes they are comprised of.

Environment

This is the physical and cultural environment of the company or organization you work for. The physical environment is your workspace: indoors in an office setting, at a restaurant or retail outlet, or outdoors at a job site or at a customer's premises. It also includes city, country, and commuting, and basic physiological needs such as air conditioning, noise pollution, and washroom access. It includes the culture of the organization, and ability to protect employees from physical and emotional harm, harassment and abuse. This Corners provides the Maslow's needs of *Physiology* and *Safety*.

Attributes:
- *Physical Safety:* This is safety from accidents and violence. This includes training and policies related to physical safety.
- *Emotional Safety:* This is safety from abuse, discrimination, bias and bullying.
- *Ergonomics:* This addresses the design and comfort of your workstation/area/machine and tasks.
- *Culture:* This refers to the social climate of your work environment. It covers the ability of the organization to receive and act on feedback, and how enjoyable and fun the work atmosphere is.
- *Location:* This takes into account all levels of physical location: part of town, rural, city, and country. It includes proximity to family and friends, and convenience of commuting.

Compensation

This is what you get for what you do - salary or hourly wages, benefits, company equity, bonuses, and non-monetary reward such as job flexibility. The physiology need comes from compensation paying for things like food and shelter. Being compensated very well or poorly can affect your sense of esteem. This Cornerstone provides the Maslow's needs of *Physiology* and *Esteem*.

Attributes:
- **Base Pay:** This is the basic pay you receive, hourly, weekly, yearly.
- **Benefits:** This refers to any and all benefits, from healthcare to things such as personal use of company resources and company discounts.
- **Overtime Pay:** This is how adequately employees are compensated for working extra hours.
- **Bonus Pay:** This refers to discretionary bonuses paid out by your organization.
- **Work Hours Flexibility:** This is the ability to adjust your work hours to accommodate your life issues. It includes flexible workday start-finish times, ability to take time off for personal issues and replace with other hours (like weekends, for instance). It also includes the ability to work from home when appropriate.

Relationships

This encompasses all relationships and relationship characteristics of those you interact with: Co-workers, managers, suppliers, customer engagement, plus your relationship with the company as a whole. Esteem is provided by the respect and status provided to you from those you interact with at work. This Cornerstone maps to the Maslow needs of Belonging and Esteem.

Attributes:
- **Manager:** This is your relationship to the person who directs your work priorities and evaluates your performance.
- **Co-Worker:** This is any and all individuals who work for the

same organization that you interact with.

- *Customer:* These are customers of your organization that you interact with.
- *Supplier:* These are suppliers to your organization that you interact with.
- *Organization:* This is your relationship to the organization as a whole, from its ability to provide you support.

Nature

The nature of your job is what you do at work - the tasks you perform, the skills you develop, use, and exhibit, the responsibilities you hold. The Cornerstone is the contributor to the Maslow need of Self-Actualization.

Attributes:
- *Assignments/Tasks:* These are the activities you do at your job. It can be equipment operation, cleaning, office tasks, sales, project management, etc.
- *Responsibilities:* This is the level of authority and responsibility you have at work. You may be responsible just for your tasks, or you could be a manager, or have responsibility for a business segment (like inventory).
- *Development Opportunities:* This refers to what your organization offers you in terms of training and skills development, and ability to be promoted to higher responsibilities and compensation.
- *Support for Initiatives:* This is how your organization responds to your suggestions related to improving your organization's efficiency, productivity, profitability - anything that reflects your interest in going above and beyond to improve things where you work.
- *Organization Competence:* This refers to how proud you are of the organization that employs you. This includes how good

your organization is at doing what it's set up to do, how you feel about what it does, and how it goes about its activities (ethics).

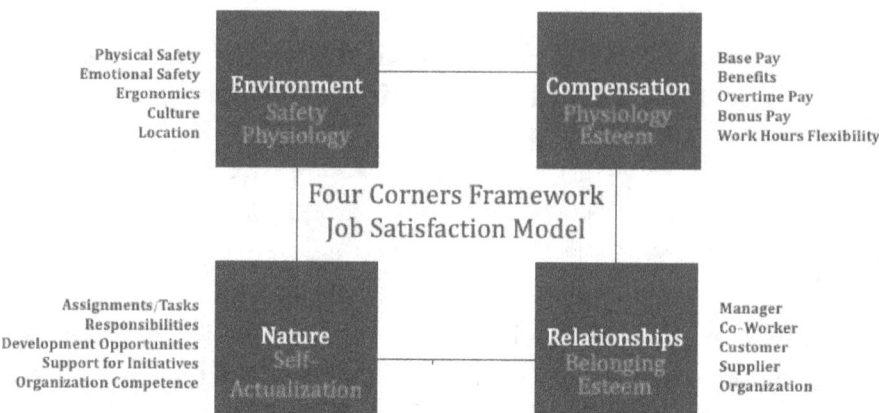

You can see from this that your job satisfaction boils down to no more than *twenty* fundamental attributes (and probably less, as you will see), organized under *Four Cornerstone* categories, driven by the five fundamental Maslow needs. Assessing the individual attributes identifies the specific issues you must work to resolve or improve to move from unsatisfied to satisfied, and beyond to engaged. The Four Corners analysis provides additional insight into what you value at work and how well that is being met. This is the self-awareness needed to be able to engineer your job and work environment to your liking, and properly assess future jobs and work environments you might consider. Next, we will go through how to create this self-assessment, and importantly how to act on it.

CHAPTER 4: THE FOUR CORNERS FRAMEWORK SELF-ASSESSMENT PROCESS

"Knowing yourself is the beginning of all wisdom"
Aristotle

Now that we've built a model to help us understand our job satisfaction, we need the input into the model - the Self-Assessment - to run the model and get the output. The output will be a complete picture of what we value in our job, displaying simultaneously the problem bits alongside the parts we enjoy, unclouded from the parts that are not valued. This then gives us the clarity to begin improvement efforts.

The Process

There are twenty job attributes in the *Self-Assessment Process*. You will find that for your specific job and circumstances only a portion of the twenty will be meaningful to you. Only two decisions need to be made for each of these:

1. The importance of the job attribute to you: How do you *value* this attribute to you?
2. The rating of the job attribute: How **satisfied**

are you with it in your job today?

The Personal Value Of A Job Attribute

You will recall that we derived our definition of *Satisfaction* from fulfilling Needs, Expectations, and Wishes:

The fulfillment of those things we deem are essential, those things that we believe strongly that we deserve, and those things that we desire or hope for.

The way we value an attribute therefore is to assign it as a *Need*, an *Expectation*, or a *Wish*.:

<u>A Need</u> *is something we require NOW because it is essential or very important.*
<u>An Expectation</u> *is a strong belief that something will happen or be the case in the future (a future Need).*
<u>A Wish</u> *is a strong desire or hope for something that is not easily attainable (a hopeful Need).*

Valuing the attributes of your job in this way is something that you've never been asked to do before - assess each of them not just as you see today, but also how they fit into your future plans and hopes. We all try to do our jobs to the best of our ability today - meet the demands of our organization, our manager, our family, ourselves. But we also spend time imagining the tomorrow of our job, and we do it regularly. The value assignment helps us clarify what aspects of our job are for today, and what are for our future.

Sorting job attributes into Needs, Expectations and Wishes is the most challenging part of the Four Corners Framework Self-Assessment Process. What we value from our work will be influenced by those around us: parents, friends, peers - even children! It is influenced by where we are in our career: beginning, middle or end. It is influenced by what our specific current life circumstances are. One person in your situation might value a certain attribute very highly, while another may not value it at all.

It is important to do this step with deliberation, at a time where you are able to be introspective and focused. Is it really honest to say this attribute is a Need NOW? Are you being reasonable and objective when you say that attribute is a reasonable Expectation from your job? Maybe you're being too modest in saying this other attribute is only a Wish?

Remember, any attribute can also be deemed "Not Relevant" if you feel that's the case. Establishing what *is not important* to you in your job is just as significant as what is important. You may find that this self-assessment process reveals to you some truths that have been hard to admit - that you are frustrated with some aspect of your job that you have assumed is important but really isn't. Maybe you are unsatisfied with an attribute of your job that only matters to you because of peer pressure, parental pressure, or some unidentified insecurity. Maybe the frustration with not getting that promotion evaporates when you admit to yourself that the reason was that you never truly valued it anyway. Unburdening yourself from chasing attributes that you do not value at all can not only be immediately gratifying but can refocus wasted energy on attributes you truly care about.

Be patient with yourself in this process. You may need a couple of revisions of your list before you feel it truly reflects *you* rather than all that influences you.

Rating a Job Attribute

Having identified the attributes, we value and how we value them, the next step is to assign a measure of satisfaction to each. There are three simple levels to choose from:

Unsatisfied ⇆ *Satisfied* ⇆ *Very Satisfied*

To help with this decision each job attribute has a description of two simple states. These states are referred to as the **Good** state and the **Bad** state of the attribute. These descriptions are provided as guidance in understanding your level of satisfaction with the attribute.

For example, let us consider the **Relationship Cornerstone** attribute **Co-Workers**. The two states of this attribute are:

> **Good:**
> "Good communication, cooperation, openness, mutual respect, trust"

> **Bad:**
> "Poor communication, cooperation and openness, lack of mutual respect, no trust"

These definitions should be helpful but recognize that they are not rigid. It is important in the assessment to trust your state of mind. If you look at an attribute and immediately feel unsatisfied with it, **you are unsatisfied**. If you're unsure how to rate it, then mark it **Satisfied**. We want this process to point out the unambiguous areas to focus on for improvement - those that are rated **Unsatisfied** and **Very Satisfied** will establish what urgently needs to be worked on, and what we love about our job that justifies the effort.

Let's look at some examples. We will start with the first attribute in the **Environment Cornerstone, Physical Safety**. Recall that the definition is:

> **Physical Safety:** This is safety from accidents and violence. This includes training and policies related to physical safety.

Do you see this attribute valued as a **Need**, and **Expectation**, or a **Wish** for you in your current job? This may seem obviously a **Need** for any job. To be able to do a job properly one must feel that they are appropriately protected from physical harm while doing it.

Assessing the **Rating** for this attribute may be a little less obvious. If you are an office worker, you can fully expect that you shouldn't fear for your life every time you sit at your desk. If you are worried about building security, threatening co-workers or poor emergency evacuation procedures, you would rate this **Unsatisfied**.

If you operate heavy construction equipment as a career, though, there is obviously a greater risk of personal harm. How about policing, firefighting, or emergency rescue? Physical risk is Intrinsic to these jobs. In these cases, your rating should be concerned about things like emergency procedures, equipment design, or training of yourself or co-workers so that the risk is properly minimized.

In this example the individual valued the attribute is rated a Need, and Unsatisfied "...because of insufficient training on the equipment I operate."

Let's try a second example from the **Nature Cornerstone: Responsibilities**. Recall the definition is:

> **Responsibilities:** This is the level of authority and responsibility you have at work. You may be responsible just for your tasks, or you could be a manager, or have responsibility for a business segment (like inventory)

If you are an ambitious individual and you are overdue for advancement at your job you could view the **Responsibilities** attribute as a **Need**.

Alternatively, you may feel that you have been building the skills to be trusted to acquire greater responsibilities in the near future, making it an **Expectation**.

You may see that you are not currently on a path to be considered for more responsibilities, but very much like the fact that with the right steps - training, performance - this could be a possibility in the future, hence it is a **Wish**.

You can see from this how the process sets your improvement direction. If it is a *Need* then it must be urgently addressed. If it is an *Expectation,* then there must be focus on it in the short term. If it's a *Wish,* then you must form a plan to develop it into an *Expectation* before it is realized.

In this example the attribute is rated an Expectation, and Very Satisfied "... because I'm being given the training to adopt more responsibilities in the near future, which will meet my income goals."

Job Satisfaction Self-Assessment Form

Enough theory - time to do some real work! The *Self-Assessment Form* is one page of information collection. You can step through the sections and record your answers on a sheet of paper.

The easy steps are:

- Read the *Good* and *Bad* states for guidance on rating
- Select how you value the attribute
- Select how you rate the attribute for ones that you *do not* label "Not Relevant"

I recommend that you take notes on your decisions along the way. From this information our next step will be to build the *Transition Plan* - moving to a more *Satisfied* and *Engaged* work experience!

CHAPTER 5: SELF-ASSESSMENT INTERPRETATION AND FOUR CORNERS INSIGHT

"Your vision will become clear only when you can look into your own heart. Who looks outside, dreams, who looks inside, awakes."

Carl Jung

As we move into the interpretation of the *Four Corners Self-Assessment*, recognize that fundamental to this entire book is the goal of creating awareness. Awareness of what you value in your job, awareness of what your job should be contributing to your life in general. Awareness of what you can influence that you didn't think you could. This should empower you. While the book offers you a process for acting on this new insight, none of this is rigid. As the process illuminates some things you might not have previously considered, or instigates some new thinking or optimism, you have the freedom to approach this in any way that you feel comfortable with. Don't be constrained by process!

Let us first take a look at an example filled out *Four Corners Self-Assessment Form*. This figure shows the format, and the basic instructions for how to fill it out:

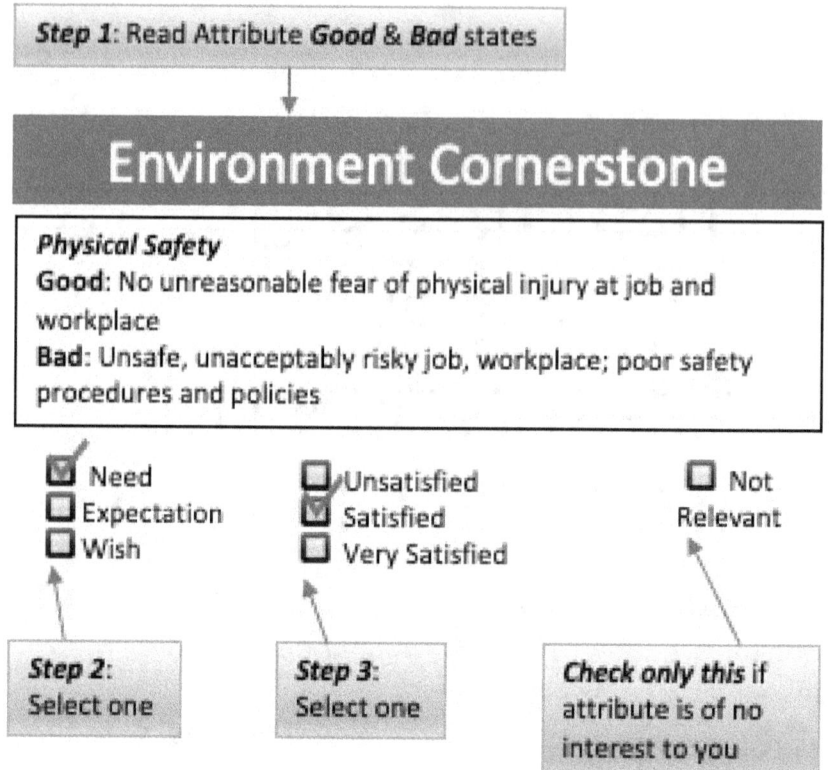

The following images show the form (abbreviated) filled out. Colors have been used for the attribute ratings - green for Very Satisfied, blue for Satisfied, and red for Unsatisfied:

Category	Item	Need	Expectation	Wish	Unsatisfied	Satisfied	Very Satisfied	Not Relevant
Environment	Physical Safety	☑	☐	☐	☐	☑	☐	☐
	Emotional Safety	☑	☐	☐	☐	☑	☐	☐
	Ergonomics	☑	☐	☐	☐	☑	☐	☐
	Culture	☑	☐	☐	☑	☐	☐	☐
	Location	☑	☐	☐	☐	☐	☑	☐
Compensation	Base Pay	☐	☑	☐	☑	☐	☐	☐
	Benefits	☑	☐	☐	☐	☐	☑	☐
	Overtime Pay	☐	☐	☐	☐	☐	☐	☑
	Bonus Pay	☐	☐	☑	☐	☐	☑	☐
	Work Hours Flexibility	☐	☑	☐	☐	☐	☑	☐

Relationships

	Need	Expectation	Wish	Unsatisfied	Satisfied	Very Satisfied	Not Relevant
Manager	☑	☐	☐	☑	☐	☐	☐
Co-Workers	☑	☐	☐	☐	☐	☑	☐
Customers	☐	☐	☐	☐	☐	☐	☑
Suppliers	☐	☑	☐	☐	☑	☐	☐
Organization	☐	☑	☐	☐	☑	☐	☐

Nature

	Need	Expectation	Wish	Unsatisfied	Satisfied	Very Satisfied	Not Relevant
Assignments/Tasks	☑	☐	☐	☑	☐	☐	☐
Responsibilities	☐	☑	☐	☐	☑	☐	☐
Development Opportunities	☐	☐	☑	☑	☐	☐	☐
Support for Initiative	☐	☑	☐	☑	☐	☐	☐
Organization Competence	☐	☑	☐	☑	☐	☐	☐

Now here is blank attributes form for you to fill out. Remember to read the **Good** and **Bad** states for guidance.

Environment Cornerstone

Physical Safety
Good: No unreasonable fear of physical injury at job and workplace
Bad: Unsafe, unacceptably risky job, workplace; poor safety procedures and policies

☐ Need   ☐ Unsatisfied   ☐ Not
☐ Expectation   ☐ Satisfied   Relevant
☐ Wish   ☐ Very Satisfied

Emotional Safety
Good: Emotionally comfortable job and workplace
Bad: Bullying, racism, sexism, inappropriate sexual advances, intimidation, shunning

☐ Need   ☐ Unsatisfied   ☐ Not
☐ Expectation   ☐ Satisfied   Relevant
☐ Wish   ☐ Very Satisfied

Ergonomics
Good: Proper ergonomics including workspace, and work environment (i.e., temperature, noise, breaks, facilities, etc.)
Bad: Inadequate ergonomics, uncomfortable environment, distractions, interruptions

☐ Need   ☐ Unsatisfied   ☐ Not
☐ Expectation   ☐ Satisfied   Relevant
☐ Wish   ☐ Very Satisfied

Culture
Good: Strong culture of fairness; good conflict resolution, work-life balance, fun workdays
Bad: Biased treatment, favoritism; poor conflict resolution; constant termination fear, layoff, constant change causing disruption

☐ Need   ☐ Unsatisfied   ☐ Not
☐ Expectation   ☐ Satisfied   Relevant
☐ Wish   ☐ Very Satisfied

Location
Good: Manageable commute; acceptable town, city, country
Bad: Difficult, time-consuming, stressful commute; undesirable town, city, country

☐ Need   ☐ Unsatisfied   ☐ Not
☐ Expectation   ☐ Satisfied   Relevant
☐ Wish   ☐ Very Satisfied

Compensation Cornerstone

Base Pay
Good: Adequate competitive salary (annual, hourly wage, commission) for needs and in relation to other organizations
Bad: Underpaid based on needs or market comparisons for job

☐ Need   ☐ Unsatisfied   ☐ Not
☐ Expectation   ☐ Satisfied   Relevant
☐ Wish   ☐ Very Satisfied

Benefits
Good: Adequate benefits (health, pension, etc.) for needs, and in relation to other comparable organizations
Bad: No benefits, inadequate benefits compared to needs

☐ Need   ☐ Unsatisfied   ☐ Not
☐ Expectation   ☐ Satisfied   Relevant
☐ Wish   ☐ Very Satisfied

Overtime Pay
Good: Appropriate compensation for extra hours worked
Bad: No overtime pay, inadequate compensation for demands of extra hours or work contribution

☐ Need   ☐ Unsatisfied   ☐ Not
☐ Expectation   ☐ Satisfied   Relevant
☐ Wish   ☐ Very Satisfied

Bonus Pay
Good: Bonus pay meets expectations, market comparison
Bad: No bonus or discretionary financial incentives, inadequate compensation for extra effort or work contribution

☐ Need   ☐ Unsatisfied   ☐ Not
☐ Expectation   ☐ Satisfied   Relevant
☐ Wish   ☐ Very Satisfied

Work Hours Flexibility
Good: Work schedule flexibility meets needs (regular and periodic), comparable to market
Bad: Insufficiently flexible work schedule for needs

☐ Need
☐ Expectation
☐ Wish

☐ Unsatisfied
☐ Satisfied
☐ Very Satisfied

☐ Not
Relevant

Relationships Cornerstone

Manager
Good: Good communication, cooperation, openness, mutual respect, trust
Bad: Poor communication, cooperation and openness, lack of mutual respect, no trust

☐ Need
☐ Expectation
☐ Wish

☐ Unsatisfied
☐ Satisfied
☐ Very Satisfied

☐ Not
Relevant

Co-Workers
Good: Good communication, cooperation, openness, mutual respect, trust
Bad: Poor communication, cooperation and openness, lack of mutual respect, no trust

☐ Need
☐ Expectation
☐ Wish

☐ Unsatisfied
☐ Satisfied
☐ Very Satisfied

☐ Not
Relevant

Customers
Good: Good communication, cooperation, openness, mutual respect, trust
Bad: Poor communication, cooperation and openness, lack of mutual respect, no trust

☐ Need   ☐ Unsatisfied   ☐ Not
☐ Expectation   ☐ Satisfied   Relevant
☐ Wish   ☐ Very Satisfied

Suppliers
Good: Good communication, cooperation, openness, mutual respect, trust
Bad: Poor communication, cooperation and openness, lack of mutual respect, no trust

☐ Need   ☐ Unsatisfied   ☐ Not
☐ Expectation   ☐ Satisfied   Relevant
☐ Wish   ☐ Very Satisfied

Organization
Good: Aligned with organization, strategic direction, ethics; good communication; opportunity for feedback to organization
Bad: Mis-alignment with organization direction, ethics; poor communication; no opportunity for feedback to organization

☐ Need   ☐ Unsatisfied   ☐ Not
☐ Expectation   ☐ Satisfied   Relevant
☐ Wish   ☐ Very Satisfied

Nature Cornerstone

Assignments/Tasks

Good: Stimulating and challenging work assignments; tasks provide good motivation and work interest
Bad: Under-utilized, bored; over-utilized; stressed, overwhelmed

☐ Need   ☐ Unsatisfied   ☐ Not
☐ Expectation   ☐ Satisfied   Relevant
☐ Wish   ☐ Very Satisfied

Responsibilities

Good: Aligned with work responsibilities for role; appropriate authority
Bad: Under-utilized, underestimated or tasked beyond capability, experience, capacity

☐ Need   ☐ Unsatisfied   ☐ Not
☐ Expectation   ☐ Satisfied   Relevant
☐ Wish   ☐ Very Satisfied

Development Opportunities

Good: Appropriate development opportunities path (assignments, training, increased responsibilities)
Bad: Development stagnation; no opportunities for skills improvement; no advancement opportunities

☐ Need   ☐ Unsatisfied   ☐ Not
☐ Expectation   ☐ Satisfied   Relevant
☐ Wish   ☐ Very Satisfied

Support for Initiative

Good: Opportunities and support for taking initiative, risks that benefit the organization

Bad: Inadequate opportunities or support for taking initiative, risks that benefit the organization

---

☐ Need   ☐ Unsatisfied   ☐ Not
☐ Expectation   ☐ Satisfied   Relevant
☐ Wish   ☐ Very Satisfied

Organization

Good: Aligned with organization, strategic direction, ethics; good communication; opportunity for feedback to organization

Bad: Mis-alignment with organization direction, ethics; poor communication; no opportunity for feedback to organization

---

☐ Need   ☐ Unsatisfied   ☐ Not
☐ Expectation   ☐ Satisfied   Relevant
☐ Wish   ☐ Very Satisfied

The First Simple Interpretation Steps

Scan over your Self-Assessment for a few moments and absorb what you are telling yourself. Look down the form at attributes you have labelled a ***Need***, and how you've assessed them in your current job. Once again as a reminder, ***Needs*** are attributes you require NOW, and are non-negotiable. Any ***Need*** that you've rated ***Very Satisfied*** is something that clearly holds you to your job. It's important to appreciate that. Now, any ***Need*** listed as ***Unsatisfied*** is a "sore thumb" and will be your primary focus for improvement. Make a list of each category. Now follow the same process now for ***Expectations*** and ***Wishes***.

The Second Step - Four Corners Insight

Out of the Self-Assessment we can extract the **Four Corners Framework Personal Model** of what brings you satisfaction at work in a general sense at this point in your life. This is the link between the Framework and the Maslow Hierarchy. The way we do this is simply to make a table of attribute values grouped by **Framework Corner**.

First let's look at the example tally including just the attribute values (this table you can write out just as well):

Cornerstone	Maslow Needs	Need	Expectation	Wish	Not Relevant
		Importance			
Environment	Safety Physiology	5			
Compensation	Physiology Esteem	1	2	1	1
Relationships	Esteem Belonging	2	2		1
Nature	Self-Actualization	1	3	1	

We will look at **Needs** tally first. Since each **Cornerstone** has 5 attributes, we can see in the example that the person values all 5 attributes in **Environment** as a **Need**. This was also much higher ranked than other **Cornerstones**. We can interpret that in a very general sense **Environment** - mapping to Maslow needs of Safety and Physiology - is the most important current **Cornerstone** for this person. Recall that the attributes under **Environment** are:

Physical Safety
Emotional Safety
Ergonomics
Culture
Location

The other **Cornerstones** are spread out more towards **Expectation** and **Wish**, indicating that these are more the near and future requirements from their work. This would be consistent with someone who currently requires the basics of work to be well under control.

It's important not to draw deep conclusions with this analysis. It's merely an indication of what is most valuable to someone, and in what time frame. Keeping this simple message in mind during the rest of your Self-Assessment analysis will be a benefit.

Here is a real-life example. I know someone who recently had firm plans for early retirement. They had a good high paying job with no other serious issues. They had a bus commute from the suburbs to downtown of a major city - about 40 min. each way - but they were very organized and used to it, so it wasn't a significant factor in their daily life. Or so they thought. Once the coronavirus pandemic hit their company required most of the staff to work from home, and this went on for months. This individual found that the shift to work-from-home had a profoundly positive effect on their daily life, making both the workday and home logistics easier and more enjoyable. They now enjoyed their job enough to delay retirement and focus for a while longer on retirement savings.

This change in job satisfaction came through merely happenstance. The **Four Corners** model can reveal this proactively.

Now let's add in the attribute ratings to our table:

Cornerstone	Maslow Needs	Importance				Satisfaction		
		Need	Expectation	Wish	Not Relevant	Unsatisfied	Satisfied	Very Satisfied
Environment	Safety Physiology	5				1	3	1
Compensation	Physiology Esteem	1	2	1	1	1		3
Relationships	Esteem Belonging	2	2		1	1	2	1
Nature	Self-Actualization	1	3	1		4	1	

This shows satisfaction with the **Environment Cornerstone**, and significant dissatisfaction with the **Nature Cornerstone**. The story that emerges (remember, in very general terms) is that the future prospects of the job are a primary concern for this individual, despite being happy with the current state.

You can see how this simple analysis is providing a compass to use when navigating improvement to one's work experience. Now complete your own *Four Corners Insight* table.

Once you've spent time absorbing the input from the Self-Assessment and you've completed the Four Corners Insight table, we can move on to the process of addressing the sources of dissatisfaction that you've identified.

CHAPTER 6:
TRANSITION PLANS

"The universe doesn't give you what you ask for with your thoughts - it gives you what you demand with your actions."
Steve Maraboli

The task at hand now is to take this personal model we have and develop it into an action plan. More than that, we can develop a map that can lead all the way to *Engagement* at your job, if you so choose. The way we do this is to create for each problem attribute a *Transition Plan*.

In the *Four Corners Framework* process, *Transition* simply refers to the direction to take in changing an attribute from its *Bad* state to its *Good* state. To do this we need to explain succinctly what is causing it to be in the *Bad* state, and what describes the target *Good* state that would make us satisfied. To illustrate this let's do an example from the completed Self-Assessment form. Under the *Environment Cornerstone*, the "Culture" attribute is marked as a *Need*, and as *Unsatisfied*:

Culture

Good: Strong culture of fairness; good conflict resolution, work-life balance, fun workdays

Bad: Biased treatment, favoritism; poor conflict resolution; constant termination fear, layoff, constant change causing disruption

---

☑ Need   ☑ Unsatisfied   ☐ Not
☐ Expectation   ☐ Satisfied   Relevant
☐ Wish   ☐ Very Satisfied

Since this attribute is considered a *Need*, improving it is essential to the person's current job satisfaction. The default *Bad* state description provides a general idea of what might be wrong, but to be able to work on this we need to know more specifically what the problem is. This must be written in a simple, clear problem statement that points us to a solution. For example:

> *"The culture at my workplace is very negative and critical. The constant negativity makes it a depressing place to work."*

Using more than one or two sentences of description here can make the problem too diffuse and unsolvable, so you must work to keep it short and to the point. You may need to rewrite the problem statement once or twice to get it clear and simple.

Our next step is to create another clear statement that is our desired *Good* state. Most people *love* to just point out problems, or conclude that the only solutions available are extreme and impractical. Let's first look at a couple of **bad** examples of solution statements:

> *Example #1: "The CEO has to be fired."*

Example #2: "Everyone should improve their attitude."

These proposed **Good** states both have a few problems. First, they are too vague about what the **Good** state looks like. Secondly, they are far beyond a typical employee's sphere of influence. Changing a CEO and changing everyone's behavior would require an audacious level of workplace control! If your **Good** state descriptions involve solutions that you KNOW are out of your control and unrealistic, you are inadvertently trying to convince yourself that you are powerless to influence change.

With this in mind, a more appropriate **Good** state description might be:

> *"I need my work environment to be positive and supportive."*

First of all, this is a statement which evokes the positive feelings this employee seeks. Secondly it abandon's blame. These are both important **Good** state characteristics. A positive, blame-free goal maximizes a person's influence on the path to its achievement. Thirdly, it incorporates the word "need" in the **Good** state solution, which signifies precisely its importance to the employee.

We now have created a ***Transition Plan*** for the attribute, summarized here using a standardized format (you can of course write this out just as well):

Needs Transition Plans				
Attribute Name	Unsatisfied	Transition Plan (LEVEL 1)	Satisfied	Transition Plan (LEVEL 2) / Very Satisfied
Culture	X	**Bad:** The culture at my workplace is very negative and critical. The constant negativity makes it a depressing place to work.		**Good:**
		Good: I need my work environment to be positive and supportive.		**Best:**

This is to be done for every attribute designated a **Need**. For attributes ranked **Satisfied** we enter this in the right column of the form, and the states become **Good** and **Best**, as shown in the example below:

Needs Transition Plans				
Attribute Name	Unsatisfied	Transition Plan (LEVEL 1)	Satisfied	Transition Plan (LEVEL 2) / Very Satisfied
Physical Safety		**Bad:**	X	**Good:** All my basic needs are met regarding physical safety at work.
		Good:		**Best:** It would be great if we had some first aide training.

We work through those rated **Unsatisfied** first, then those rated **Satisfied**, then complete the table at the end with those rated **Very Satisfied**. We want to always keep this last group in our field of view because it's motivating to remind ourselves of the things we really like about our work!

You can see the **Transition Plan** moves from **Bad** to **Good** to **Best** states. If you can achieve the **Best** state, then you have reached **Very Satisfied** in your **Transition Plan**!

Once you've completed your **Needs** Transition Plans, the same thing is to be done for attributes labelled **Expectation**. When writing the **Good** or **Best** state for an **Expectation**, remember that expectations are something *imminent*, like in the near future. It must be written in a form expressing a disconnect between what you *believe* should happen, and what you currently *expect* to happen. Let's try an example again from the completed example Self-Assessment form.

The attribute **Base Pay** was labelled **Expectation**, and ranked **Unsatisfied**:

> **Base Pay**
> **Good**: Adequate competitive salary (annual, hourly wage, commission) for needs and in relation to other organizations
> **Bad**:   Underpaid based on needs or market comparisons for job

☐ Need   ☑ Unsatisfied   ☐ Not
☑ Expectation   ☐ Satisfied   Relevant
☐ Wish   ☐ Very Satisfied

The easiest way to make the solution statement for **Expectations** is to start with the words "My expectation is that..". Here is the example is the standard form:

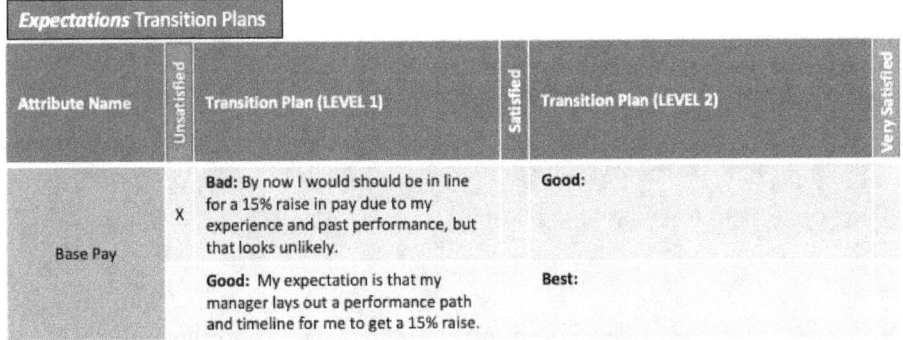

Expectations Transition Plans					
Attribute Name	Unsatisfied	**Transition Plan (LEVEL 1)**	Satisfied	**Transition Plan (LEVEL 2)**	Very Satisfied
Base Pay	X	**Bad:** By now I would should be in line for a 15% raise in pay due to my experience and past performance, but that looks unlikely.		**Good:**	
		Good: My expectation is that my manager lays out a performance path and timeline for me to get a 15% raise.		**Best:**	

If you *need* a raise it is because you are not covering your essential expenses at your current pay. If you *expect* a raise, that is because you think it's fair - you've been in the job long enough, you've worked hard enough, and the market for your skills tells you that you deserve it.

The Transition Plans for **Wishes** are treated similarly. We want

to clarify in the **Good** state for these that this is beyond expectations by starting each with "My wish is that…". Remember
that **Wishes** are things that indicate the hope of longer-term outcomes. A good organization should provide us with hopes of very
good outcomes if we seek them, even if we cannot yet see them as
being achievable in the short term. Taking from our example self-
Analysis:

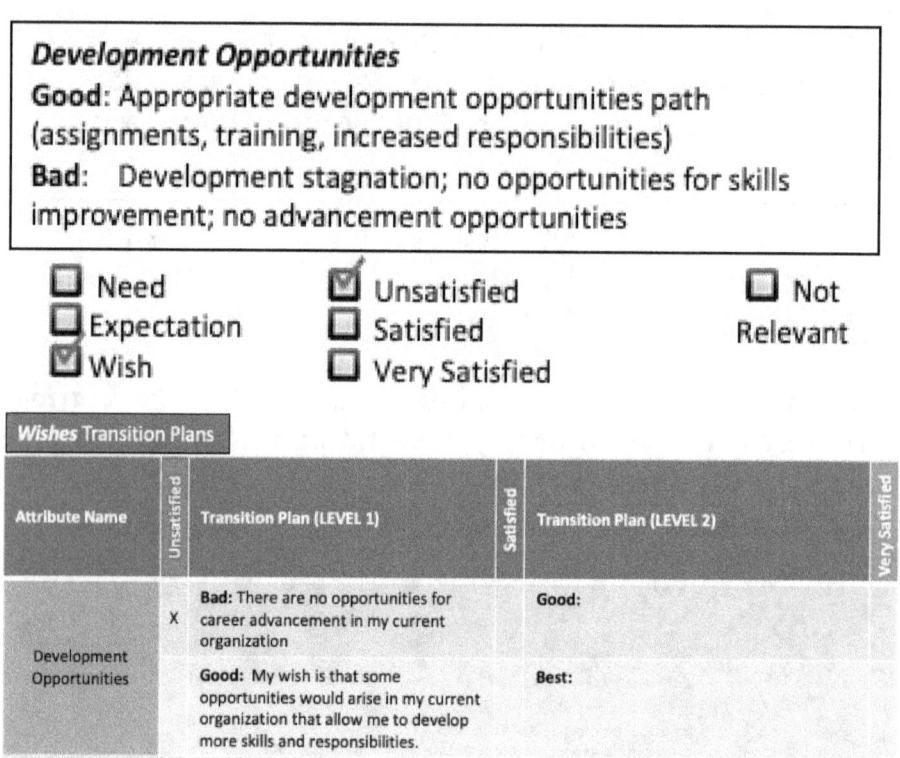

Now you can go ahead and complete the **Transition Plans** for
all of your **Needs, Expectations**, and **Wishes.** Once you're finished,
look it over and give yourself a pat on the back. You've done what
few in the world have done - taken the planning of your job satisfaction seriously. You're now ready to attack what's left of that
70,000-100,000 hours of work you'll be doing armed with an ac-
tual *plan to make it enjoyable*!

CHAPTER 7: CLOSING THE BAD STATE-GOOD STATE GAPS

"If it's never our fault we can't take responsibility for it. If we can't take responsibility for it, we'll always be its victim."
Richard Bach

The next stage of our process is to define the **specific** actions to take to close the **Bad** state-**Good** state gaps for the important attributes that have been identified. The circumstances that have *created* these gaps, and the steps to take to *close* them are going to be specific to the nature of your work, the individuals involved, and maybe most importantly, *your* personality. Providing gap-closing steps for you without intimate awareness of these details is clearly not possible. Guidance can be offered, however, on how to best approach this process.

In the effort to move important job attributes to the desired Good state, three important elements need to be included:

1. How best to **communicate** your job satisfaction needs and goals - your desired Good states - to your organization
2. How to maximize your **influence** in pushing for the changes you seek
3. How to effectively **negotiate** with your organization when the job attribute changes you re-

quire are not easily accepted

Communication

In my experience as a manager the first thing I needed from an employee struggling with job satisfaction issues was to understand clearly what the issue or issues were, and what the individual sought as a resolution. From that point we could start discussing solutions. This meant finding alignment between what I as the manager felt should, and could, be done and the employee's desired outcome. As mentioned earlier, managers have their own set of work issues causing them stress or frustration. Approaching your manager in an organized and prepared way - able to clearly articulate concerns, and proposed solutions - is a tremendously positive way to go about this. The Transition Plans you have created provide the basis for starting this process effectively.

The second thing I needed from the employee was to have them approach this interaction in a collaborative way. Too often employees come to their manager to vent and complain about their issues when they are frustrated, upset, or angry. An employee in an agitated state of mind is also commonly bringing an adversarial attitude - about the organization in general, or the manager specifically. They have already gone through the arguments and discussions in their head by themselves, and without a happy resolution. This can result in the real engagement being more a set of demands than a discussion about how to work together to make things better for the employee. The likely outcome here is obvious. Put yourself in the manager's position. If someone comes to you angry with a list of things you *must* do for them - or - if they come to you with problems and ask for your help in finding solutions, in which scenario are you best motivated to help them?

The general theme that you use when communicating your job satisfaction issues is also very important to nurturing the spirit of collaboration. When communicating your request to discuss your Transition Plan, It should be framed In words connected to your work, not just your personal happiness. Instead of saying something like:

> *"I need to talk to you about some things that are bothering me at work"*

I'd suggest - as corny as it sounds - using opening statements like:

> *"I'd like to have a discussion with you about how I can improve my focus, productivity, and effectiveness at my job"*

The reason to use this language is that it ties your personal concerns simply and directly to what the organization needs from you. You want job satisfaction so that you can be happier and better enjoy your time spent at work. This statement is merely a translation into the benefits that your organization will see from this. This puts the discussion squarely in the lap of your manager's interests and responsibilities. By doing it this way you're maximizing the opportunity for receptiveness and collaboration.

Lastly, you should approach this as a process, not an event. By process I mean that the interaction should flow basically as follows:

1. Present your manager with a request for an initial discussion
2. Have the discussion
3. Mutually complete actions coming from the discussion (this is the Transition Plan gap closure actions)
4. Conclusion of process - summary and thanks

Regarding the first step - a meeting request - you should not blind-side a manager in a hallway with a discussion of such importance. You want your manager to schedule time so that he/she has the ability to focus on what you are communicating and appreciates it as important. Preparation and structure make this process efficient and to the point.

There of course may be multiple discussions (none should be longer than 1 hour maximum), but the basic cycle of discussion followed by actions, eventually arriving at a conclusion should be maintained.

The conclusion of your process is *very* important. It should summarize what happened in writing or email - your issue, the agreed resolution, and the outcome. You should *always* thank your manager for engaging in the process, *even if the outcome is unsatisfactory to you*. This is the mature and honorable thing to do. In some cases, you may wish to escalate your issue beyond your manager - either to Human Resources or to their manager. If you choose this path, your conclusion is the opportunity to inform your manager of this intent, so they are not blindsided by it, and give them the opportunity to provide comment on that option before you proceed.

An example:

> *"Thank you for providing me with your time and input on my initiative to improve my job satisfaction.*
>
> *We discussed my issue with [attributes Bad States] and my desire to achieve [attributes Good States]. The actions we took are [action 1], [action 2], etc.*
>
> *The outcome of this activity is now [attribute Good States]. Thank you very much for your cooperation and support"*

You may feel that you are completely inexperienced in this type of interaction with your manager, and that it makes you very anxious, nervous and stressed. Firstly, recognize that this is very common. Secondly, feel free to reveal this to your manager. A good manager will help make this process more relaxed. Also, trust that the good preparation you have done will reduce your stress and anxiety, as will the use of a collaborative approach.

Way back in 1987 I came across an audio tape lecture from Jack Canfield, made famous as the author of "Chicken Soup for the Soul". The lecture is now sold as an audiobook entitled "Maximum Confidence - 10 Steps to Extreme Self-Esteem". I would encourage anyone struggling with nerves in this communication process to listen to it. One of the many good and simple advice tips that stayed with me my whole life was his quaint mantra "Oh what the heck, go for it anyway". He recommended saying this to yourself when you were overly nervous about taking action on an initiative. This lyrical statement has the effect of adding a touch of levity to the task, relieving the anxiety. It is also a reminder that these actions are not as frightening as we sometimes think at the start. https://www.audible.ca/pd/Maximum-Confidence-Audiobook/B0719CQ3L

Influence Building

One of the central messages of this book is that if you take personal responsibility for your job satisfaction and follow the right process, you have more *influence* over positive changes in your work environment than you think. The challenge is how to *maximize* your influence, and how to use it *effectively*.

Your job, whatever it is, contributes to your organization's success. Any good organization should welcome suggestions from its employees on how to make a job more effective, or productive, or more efficient. And as we've seen from the likes of Gallup's research, improving your job satisfaction contributes to these. This is the foundation of your influence. Any initiative you propose may not only accomplish this for you, but it also may end up having benefits to other employees, and the organization in general!

The first factor contributing to maximizing your influence is to *perform your job well.* If an employee is not performing well, any conversations with management will be drawn to that topic. It is the elephant in the room always. Job performance must be very good or at least adequate to talk about other things.

There are three Important per-requisites to good job performance:

- You must know very clearly what your role is, and what your responsibilities are
- You must know very clearly what the expectations are for your performance (eg, tasks to accomplish, or "deliverables")
- You must have the skills, knowledge, and experience to meet these expectations

All three of these factors require clear, unambiguous cooperation and communication between the employee and the organization. If your organization has not clarified with you your role and responsibilities, you need to ask them for that clarification. If your organization has not clarified your performance expectations, you need to ask them to provide that. If you have been put in a role where you do not have the skills, knowledge, or experience to meet the expectations you need to communicate that to your management, and they should help you acquire them - or modify the expectations.

If you have these three prerequisites solidly in place then the only remaining important contributor to job performance is motivation, and that of course comes directly from job satisfaction. If you are not clear on your job prerequisites, it's a waste of time to work on job satisfaction - you don't really know what the job is! That has to be clear in your mind first.

The second factor maximizing influence is *attitude*. Bad attitude can be demonstrated by someone whose behavior is argumentative, confrontational, disagreeable, and/or pessimistic. A person who performs well or exceptionally at the technical aspects of their job but behaves this way erases the influence that their job performance brings. Bad attitude employees can have a negative effect on coworkers and the manager, leading to diminished performance of the overall work environment.

Nobody likes working with someone who brings a bad attitude to work, but in my experience it's common that very few people will confront them about it. If you suspect that *you* have a bad attitude but are possibly unsure if it is significant, it's necessary to investigate. Try asking your co-workers and/or manager objectively what they think of your attitude. You might be surprised at the honest feedback you get by doing this.

A bad attitude at work could clearly be the result of an extended amount of time dealing with an unsatisfactory work environment. This creates a bit of a chicken-and-egg situation - to improve your job satisfaction you need the influence provided by a good attitude, but you can't improve your attitude until your job satisfaction improves. Getting traction on how to correct a bad attitude is a domain best handled by talking to trained counsellors. If it turns out the source of your attitude problems *is* your work dissatisfaction, explain this clearly to your manager in the discussion. It should only provide additional motivation for them to help you with your job satisfaction improvement process!

Negotiation

With a good communication strategy along with influence optimization, one may be surprised at how easy it is to get change in their environment on their key attributes. There may come a point where you hit an impasse on a important Bad state And you can't achieve alignment with your manager on how to move forward to improve it. This is where negotiation comes in.

I'm certainly not an expert in negotiation technique, so I will refer you to other resources for this. There are many very good resources available - books, videos, internet. One smart individual I know recommends the publication "In Business as In Life - You Don't Get What You Deserve, You Get What You Negotiate", by Chester L. Karrass.

My main advice on negotiation is that you approach it with focus on collaboration, positivity, and a win-win outcome. This negotiation is about something personal, and with an indeterminate time engagement. Preserving a good relationship with the organization/manager is a very important part of this process. In my experience good negotiating has nothing to do with tricks or manipulation. It focuses on how to convince somebody of the facts, and that your presented desired outcome is beneficial not just to the person negotiating but the recipient as well.

What if you reach a firm impasse on a desired Good State? Consider asking what things or actions need to be put in place for that Good State to be achieved, with no consideration to the limits of the current circumstances. The things or actions may seem impossible at first, but now the impasse is broken down to bite-sized elements, each of which can be analyzed and challenged. As a minimum this requires your organization/manager to give the subject more serious thought, just in case the rejection of your proposed outcome was originally met with a flippant negative response. This path may require you to redefine an attribute from a Need or Expectation to an Expectation or a Wish. Your patience and reasonable approach may be rewarded by an earlier-than-expected return to discussion by your manager with a bit of good fortune, or creative thinking - I've seen it happen!

CHAPTER 8: THOUGHTS ON ATTRIBUTES

"Your present circumstances don't determine where you can go, they only determine where you start."

Nido R. Qubein

The following is a reitternation of the Cornerstone and Attribute definitions, and my general thoughts on the twenty attributes. Hopefully these provide you with ideas when formulating your Transition Plans.

Environment Cornerstone - Definition

This is the physical and cultural environment of the company or organization you work for. The physical environment is your workspace: indoors in an office setting, at a restaurant or retail outlet, or outdoors at a job site or at a customer's premises. It also includes city, country, and commuting and basic physiological needs such as air conditioning, noise pollution, washroom access. It includes the culture of the organization, and ability to protect employees from physical and emotional harm, harassment and abuse.

This provides the Maslow's needs of Physiology and Safety.

Attributes
Physical Safety

This is safety from accidents and violence. This includes training and policies related to physical safety.

Emotional Safety

This is safety from abuse, discrimination, bias and bullying.

Ergonomics

This addresses the design and comfort of your workstation/area/ machine and tasks.

Culture

This refers to the social climate of your work environment. It covers the ability of the organization to receive and act on feedback, and how enjoyable and fun the work atmosphere is.

Location

This takes into account all levels of physical location: part of town, rural, city, and country. It includes proximity to family and friends, and convenience of commuting.

General

Dissatisfaction with job attributes in the Environment Cornerstone might seem less important to your overall job satisfaction than attributes from other corners. Is the comfort of that chair you sit in all day all that bad? Aren't you being too fussy complaining about the workplace temperature, or the cleanliness of the washrooms and coffee station? What do you mean you don't feel that "safe" at work?

It's important to keep in mind that the Environment Cornerstone provides the Maslow's needs of Physiology and Safety - the first two steps in the Maslow pyramid. These are the Basic level, and as such most people should value them in the Four Corners Framework process as *Needs*. Comfort and satisfaction with the physiological and safety aspects at work eliminates these as fundamental distractions to your job. Shouldn't this be important to your organization?

Correspondingly, solutions to Environment attribute problems can be among the easiest problems to garner support from your organization on, and therefore the easiest to implement. Getting a quick win or two on Environment attributes can build your confidence to attack the more complex and challenging "high profile" ones!

Physical Safety Attribute
Physical Safety is not just about the immediate risks at your desk or work site. It also includes things such as safe business travel and safe travel accommodation. If you need to walk through a dark alley at night in a sketchy neighborhood to get to the entrance of your employer, that can be considered unsafe. If you have concerns about the health risks in your work environment, this is unsafe.

Physical Safety does not mean that all jobs should be risk-free, however. Your job may have intrinsic risks and danger, such as those associated with firefighting, policing, military, power line servicing, etc. There are many careers that face this. Your organization must take appropriate safety steps to protect the health of its employees. This means adequate equipment, procedures, training, and ergonomics. In most cases this is required by your local workplace safety legislation.

Pursuing clarity about Physical Safety at work means developing an understanding that your concerns are reasonable, and that you are clear on any steps that your organization has already taken to address them. If after this reflection and investigation there remains a meaningful concern, be clear that your organization should welcome you bringing forward this concern. You are trying to eliminate a real or perceived risk to you and possibly others and make your organization aware of a potential liability. This could even be affecting productivity of others at your workplace who haven't yet summoned the courage to raise the issue themselves.

You may be saying "I and others have pointed this out many times, but the manager or organization doesn't care". If the way that has been done was informal, brief, accusatory, verbal, and largely unsupported with facts then it is not necessarily surprising that it hasn't been taken seriously. Strong managers will respond quickly and decisively to *any* safety concerns expressed in *any* way because they understand the implications of an incident occurring. Average or weak managers may be indecisive, see this as something to put on their to-do list for "when they have time", or worse - view informal complaints as more time spent on bureaucracy. Owning the problem here means that you MUST carry the problem until you get an acceptable solution. This is the time to be persistent, but don't forget to do it while maintaining positivity!

Things to Consider:

- Addressing a safety concern in writing (paper or email) establishes it as a formal concern. Your organization should be motivated to respond formally, as this puts it in a precarious legal situation if a safety breach occurs.
- Approach this concern collaboratively. Instigating defensiveness will take focus away from what should be a straightforward solution.
- If you can, consider offering to coordinate or contribute to the solution (like organize a training session, or search for solutions to be considered).

Emotional Safety Attribute

Feeling emotionally threatened can be incredibly destabilizing and stressful, not only affecting job performance and satisfaction, but personal health as well. Everyone should be able to work at their job absent feelings of this sort of threat. Many companies recognize this, and now publish policy guidelines defining the expectations for this in their workplace.

This is an area of workplace culture that has evolved considerably over the last 30 years. What is defined as an emotionally safe workplace environment is also still rapidly changing. Objectively defining all things that could be considered a threat to someone's Emotional Safety under this dynamic circumstance is daunting. My approach to this is simple: If a person honestly feels emotionally threatened, then they are. The only question is what to do about it.

At one end of the spectrum, threats to Emotional Safety via bullying, racism, sexism or inappropriate advances are clear and unambiguous. At the other end the experience may be quite subtle and subjective. Recognize that individuals from different cultures and upbringing may be naive about the implications of their actions or words.
There are plenty of internet resources you can access to understand the definitions of workplace bullying, racism, sexism or inappropriate advances. There may also be resources in your company and community as well, such as help lines or counselling. Look to your organization for policy statements and help with interpretation. These can help you build confidence that you are experiencing something that needs to be addressed.

I list two categories of threats to Emotional Safety, which I refer to as "Direct" or "Bystander". Definitions are as follows:

Direct
This is bullying, racism, sexism, or inappropriate sexual advances directly targeted at you. Examples of this would be direct communication with you (verbal, electronic, or written message) involving threats, insults, racist or sexist language, or aggressive sexual advances.

A Direct threat needs to be acted on immediately. This means that Human Resources (HR) or management absolutely needs to be informed of it, and they should address this directly with the perpetrator(s). They should NOT advise you how to handle it. Telling you to "Just ignore them", or "Have you tried talking to them about how you feel to get this to stop?" is not at all acceptable. You are there to do your job, not manage the behavior of people that are crossing a line. You also should not be required to participate in the confrontation with the perpetrator. You can also expect that your complaint is communicated to the perpetrator(s) as being from an anonymous source, if that is possible.

Bystander
This is bullying, racism, sexism, or inappropriate sexual advances that you witness being targeted at someone you work with. Examples of this would be witnessing direct communication (verbal, electronic, or written message) with a co-worker involving threats, insults, racist or sexist language, or aggressive sexual advances.
Bystander incidents can raise the questions "This isn't directly affecting me, so is this really my responsibility to get involved, and how much trouble should I put myself through in raising this?" If it is troubling you, it is distracting you from performing at your job at least. Your work environment presents a situation where you are required to work and interact with individuals to accomplish tasks. Conflict is distraction, and distraction reduces productivity. Productivity and reputation are important to your organization, and it is a strong justification for your organization to deal with behavior that does not belong in, or outside, of work. There are resources here again that you can use to educate yourself on this subject. "Defender Self-Efficacy" is a standard term to search for and is the belief in one's ability to act effectively on essentially Indirect Emotional Safety threats.

It is important to raise here the circumstances where you are working with individuals that have behavioral challenges, such as intellectual disability or autism. Your Emotional Safety can be still threatened nonetheless, and the steps and desired outcome can be unchanged. It may however require more patience, understanding and compassion during the process of achieving the desired outcome.

Things to Consider:

- Addressing an Emotional Safety concern in writing (paper or email) establishes it as a formal concern. Your organization should be motivated to respond formally, as this puts it in a precarious legal situation if a safety breach occurs.
- Prepare your communication so that you can describe the situation clearly and concisely. Approach this concern collaboratively. Instigating defensiveness will take focus away from what should be a straightforward solution.
- Definitions of what constitutes offensive behaviour varies widely. Give thought to the possibility that the individual in question may need education, not punishment.

Ergonomics Attribute

Poor Ergonomics affects your ability to physically do your job efficiently and comfortably. This is quite a broad area, including things like desk setup, proper equipment availability and operation, workplace noise, temperature, or even fresh air flow.

Workplace comfort and freedom from distraction can mean very different things if you are an office worker at a desk or a security guard at a football game. You shouldn't be uncomfortably cold in either job for instance, but one means a furnace setting and air flow and the other means proper clothing. Reasonable ergonomics expectations can also be very different if you work for a multinational corporation or a local small business. Multinationals have the resources to spend money on workplace ergonomics evaluations and setups, while small businesses may only have the option of home-made inexpensive fixes.

It is common to hear people complain about their ergonomic struggles at work, and that their organization doesn't do anything about it. Ergonomics problem solutions may appear more straightforward after you take the steps of positive investigation, consultation, and discussions. You may need to coordinate these yourself in an organization that has limited resources and support. Maybe you can do something about it yourself. If so, then why suffer the frustration of the problem just because you feel the organization should solve it?

Things to Consider:

- Be open to, and search for, creative solutions. Some ergonomics problems can be expensive to solve, and that may be a challenge for a small organization.
- Investigate solutions before you start the Communication. Going in with solutions, even if they are not the best ideas, shows that you are cooperative and reasonable.
- Investigate workplace legislation in your area, and your benefits plan. These may clarify acceptable solutions for the type of problem you are experiencing.

Culture Attribute

As was stated earlier, a Bad workplace Culture is basically an unpleasant place to work. Maybe it has a lot of people complaining. Maybe coworkers are generally unfriendly. It could be that teamwork is poor or non-existent. Management may be overbearing and insensitive. Or maybe it's all of this.

While you may not be able to change the whole organization by yourself, you may be able to set a higher standard of behaviour for yourself and those you work closest with. For instance, you might find that people are less comfortable complaining in your presence if you change the subject to something positive, or even politely declare that you'd prefer to hear only constructive talk. It might be hard to help that person at work that is selfish and unhelpful, but you will break down barriers by demonstrating teamwork above trivialities. Even bitter and difficult managers can be temporarily stunned by acts of kindness, especially if they persist over time. Nobody likes to work in a culture of negativity - not even the main perpetrators. By demonstrating that you at least are above this you will show leadership to others of the same mind who are just a little less courageous to set a new trend of behaviour.

One caution in this approach however: behaving positively is good but acting as the hall monitor for good behavior - criticizing others that don't follow your example - is very bad. The natural tendency of those not behaving well is to criticize, and you could very well become a target of that. It's much harder to criticize good people who focus on their own personal behavior.

A special subject for 2020 and beyond is what I call "e-culture", or "electronic culture". This is when your workplace is partly or entirely made up of individuals working remotely. In this case interaction is not face-to-face, but through video meetings and telephone communication. While remote interactions have been going on for decades in the business world, it has only recently become more prevalent as a result of the Coronavirus pandemic. This new interaction format is likely to grow over time for people whose work can be done without direct face-to-face interaction.

A good deal of e-culture behavioral courtesies and expectations are intuitive. Some are not. In an office people can look at you to see if you're busy, or receptive to interaction. if you are working remotely that may need to be established electronically, like marking yourself as "do not disturb" on your communication software. Working from home can be a lonelier experience, and there will be people who will look to fill that void by constant instant messaging. This can be very disruptive to concentration and focus if you have detailed tasks to perform. It is worthwhile suggesting an open discussion with your team about what acceptable behaviours and protocols should be followed.

Things to Consider:

- Addressing culture problems at work does not have to wait for a top-down solution. Individuals at the working level can demonstrate incredible leadership by setting the standards they wish to live by and encouraging others to join them.
- A typical problem with bad culture is that nobody has taken the initiative, or has the courage, to show leadership to instigate change.
- It's important to approach this issue with the utmost of positivity and constructive thinking. In a bad culture organization most people know that it exists. Coming in to complain about it instead of coming with solutions may just be met with eye rolls.
- The alternative to suggesting changes that will help the environment is really just to isolate yourself as much as possible. Maintain a positive attitude yourself, politeness, and interact as little as possible to keep yourself sane.

Location Attribute

When we think about work location we think of course about the distance between home and work, and what that effect that has on commuting - time commitment, hassle, and cost. But work location can also define the distance between us and family and friends. The effect this has on our job satisfaction can be very general. This of course can be a sacrifice we need to make for a good job or a career.

Addressing Location dissatisfaction requires some careful thought and analysis. Take time to identify the specific sources of dissatisfaction and what are the best solutions. Recognize that the solution to your problem may set a precedent in your organization, so the organization has to consider the solution implications thoroughly.

Things to Consider:
- Flexible start and finish times to optimize commuting.
- Is there a possibility of working longer hours and fewer days to reduce the number of commuting cycles?
- is work-from-home a possibility.
- Consider solutions under your control: Maybe public transit instead of driving allows you to be somewhat productive in your commute; Are you making good use of your personal time - weekends and holidays - so you stay connected with family and friends to reduce the sense of separation.

Compensation Cornerstone - Definition

This is what you get for what you do - salary or hourly wages, benefits, company equity, bonuses, and non-monetary reward such as job flexibility. The physiology need comes from Compensation paying for things like food and shelter. Being compensated very well or poorly can affect your sense of esteem.

This provides the Maslow's needs of Physiology and Esteem.

Attributes
Base Pay
This is the basic pay you receive, hourly, weekly, yearly.
Benefits
This refers to any and all benefits, from healthcare to things such as personal use of company resources and company discounts.
Overtime Pay
This is how adequately employees are compensated for working extra hours.
Bonus Pay
This refers to discretionary bonuses paid out by your organization.
Work Hours Flexibility
Flexible workday start-finish times, ability to take time off for personal issues, ability to work from home when appropriate.

General
In the book we discussed the definitions of Satisfaction and Engagement. They were defined in terms of agreement between an employee and an organization that involves the exchange of value. The company seeks the value of the employee's work, and the employee in most cases looks for financial remuneration, which in turn meets the Maslow needs of *physiology* and *esteem*.

Compensation will almost always be tied tightly to performance - greater contribution should garner greater compensation. In some cases, however an organization might constrain financial compensation to disconnect this, like creating salary or raise caps, or freezes. Under these circumstances one must think about creative sources of compensation if you feel unsatisfied in general with this Cornerstone.

If we are paid well for what we do, we reap a sense of pride and importance from that. In contrast to this, if we are under compensated there's a sense of being taken advantage of, and disrespect. One part of the compensation discussion therefore is very technical - the value exchange. The other is very emotional. Recognize where your dissatisfaction lies to effectively seek and communicate solutions.

Base Pay Attribute
In most organizations, managers have very limited ability to adjust employee base pay. Changes in base pay are typically tied to organization budget cycles, which are usually on an annual schedule. Budgets will also be affected by performance of the organization. If you are in a small organization, there's obviously more flexibility if you're dealing directly with the owner. For medium or large organizations, the financial structure and formality of the business or organization financial planning provides constraints as to how compensation can be adjusted and when. This constraint notwithstanding, organizations all have the opportunity to do what they need to do in desperate circumstances. If a critical resource threatens to leave without a compensation change, accommodations can usually be made.

Throughout this book the assumption is made that we are not playing in the domain of ultimatums. This means that if we have a concern about our base pay the absolute best way to handle it is to plan to intercept the cycle most opportune for the organization to make the changes.

Compensation is broken up into five separate attributes to create awareness that these are all forms of contributing to an employee's compensation and need to be valued by the employee. In trying to increase compensation it's helpful to realize that one avenue may be difficult to get movement on while another is not. The end result may meet your objective.

Things to consider:

- Be proactive and time your request for an increase in base pay to align with your organization's review cycle.
- Do your homework. Approaching your manager for a pay raise just because you want one that's not very compelling. Come to your discussion with a few facts in hand: what do people doing a similar job get paid, and is it different from what you are getting? check your info are you contributing effectively to the organization's goals? Have you taken on more responsibility since the last time you were given a pay raise?
- Approach pay raise discussions the same way you approach annual reviews - as a negotiation. you are trying to get the best deal that you can, but at the same time have a positive, constructive discussion about it.

Benefits Attribute

Benefits are something that is typically negotiated at a group level, so an individual has very little purchase in trying to ask for specialized benefits standard benefits such as health or dental care. Benefits should as well be looked at beyond just these typical ones.

Things to consider:

- Translate benefits increase your seeking in dollars per year. This is helpful in the discussion when drawing comparisons to other companies or similar jobs that offer more benefits than yours.

- In a small company without a benefits offering, it might be possible to get the concept
  initiated. It may take some time dedication
  to organize other employees, and research
  effort.

Overtime Pay Attribute

If you are an hourly employee your compensation for hours
worked over a standard work week should be covered under legislation. The situation for salaried employees is more variable.
Some organizations see extra hours contribution - either regularly or under special circumstances - as part of the unspoken
agreement with the employee. The employee is expected (within
reason) to commit time until the job is done, and in return the
organization doesn't expect a "clock to be punched", meaning
that they are flexible with work hours spent at slower periods.
In addition, extra time commitment is viewed as demonstration
of commitment to the job and organization, and can be rewarded
with better salary increases, promotions, etc.

Things to consider:

- Try not to fall into the situation where you
  feel that there is an "unspoken arrangement"
  - that you will put in extra hours and then expect a big raise or bonus payout.
- Clarifying compensation for extra hours
  worked is best done proactively. If you are
  trying to get paid for time already spent with
  no prior "meeting of the minds" with your
  manager, it will be difficult. Have a discussion *prior* to the next event to form an alignment in expectations.
- Consider creative compensation where sim-

ple dollars payout reaches some sort of impasse - time off work, broader recognition of effort (reputation), organization perquisites.

Bonus Pay Attribute

Bonus pay can be a highly discretionary form of compensation. This can make it a nice surprise for employees when unexpected. It can also be a big negative when the manager/organization handles it poorly. The negative can come when there are expectations around the bonus that are not met, or it is perceived to be awarded unfairly.

Bonuses can also come and go with the organization's performance. Some organizations tie bonuses directly to performance metrics.

Things to consider:

- Clarifying bonus criteria must be done proactively. This allows you to align your performance to the bonus expectations, and even do periodic sensing with your manager to see if you are on track for the reward you expect.
- You may consider trying to negotiate a personal bonus compensation when attempts to increase base pay fail. This type of compensation can be tied directly to effort to meeting an organization's goals, like sales, customer service metrics, or throughput.
- Consider creative compensation where simple dollars payout reaches some sort of impasse - time off work, broader recognition of effort (reputation), organization perquisites.

Work Hours Flexibility

Work Hours Flexibility can be a tremendous compensation if

handled effectively. While managers are usually highly constrained giving out monetary compensation, many managers have formal or informal discretion to offer additional hours or days off work with pay.

Things to consider:

- Recognize that this form of compensation can be highly informal, and at a manager's discretion. As such it must be carefully used by the manager. He/she has to be careful that they are not setting presidents they cannot fulfill or creating a "shadow compensation scheme" that eventually might land them in hot water.
- Work hour flexibility is excellent retroactive compensation for extra work effort. Much easier than trying to negotiate overtime or bonus pay.

Relationships Cornerstone - Definition

This encompasses all relationships and relationship characteristics of those you interact with: Co-workers, managers, suppliers, customer engagement, plus your relationship with the company as a whole. Esteem is provided by the respect and status provided to you from those you interact with at work.

This maps to the Maslow needs of Belonging and Esteem.

Attributes
Manager
This is your relationship to the person who directs your work priorities and evaluates your performance.
Co-Workers
This is any and all individuals who work for the same organization that you interact with.
Customers
Customers of your organization or your department that you provide service to (including internal to your organization).
Suppliers
People that supply goods and/or services to your organization or department that you interact with
Organization
This is your relationship to the organization as a whole, from its ability to provide you support.

General
Organizations are made up of people, people value relationships, and therefore relationships are of tremendous importance at work. It's hard to overestimate this. Considering how much time we spend at work the relationships we have there can be a very important part of our day, even if these relationships are never extended to our personal time. Building good relationships in an organization not only benefits an individual during their working time there but can have a positive influence throughout their

career as they depend on these relationships for references and for job and career contacts.

Dissatisfaction with relationships can be a complex issue. Is there direct personality conflicts? Lack of trust? Unappealing behavior? Absolutely key to improving relationships is the ability to take personal responsibility for finding and driving the implementation of solutions. Some people may find this difficult to accept, but your ability to approach a relationship differently to make it less of a problem for you is significantly easier than trying to change another individual.

Manager Attribute
Probably the most important attribute of the 20 that I have identified is the manager relationship. More people complain about their manager than any other complaints that I've heard. Correspondingly, if an individual has a good manager it makes a tremendous difference in their work environment, and their loyalty to their organization. This is understandable because of the manager's influence on an employee's life. The day-to-day assignments, compensation, even influence over one's long-term career path all depend on the manager.

Often people I talk to have a difficult time thinking of their manager as simply a human being, with comparable work stresses and challenges. This can lead to a complete loss of empathy for their manager, which certainly compromises the ability to have a good relationship with them.

Things to consider:
- You must identify specific, measurable, addressable issues to work on to improve your relationship. generalities won't get you anywhere.
- If you are having a difficult time aligning with your manager on how to do something,

or what is considered a quality job, consider looking at your manager more like a customer of your work. This may make it less a battle for control, and more a question of education (both ways).

- Remember that your manager is in a position of more control because they have more responsibility. With more responsibility comes more risk in the case of failure. This can lead to them being more demanding instead of seeking collaboration. Identify where they see risks and deal with that instead of debating approaches.

- Whether you like your manager or not, your approach should always be to work to make them successful. This will benefit you as well. Whether you feel your manager is competent or not, you must work to build their trust, and they will trust you only if they see that you are sincerely on their side. The more they trust you the more they will listen to your advice and your input.

Coworkers Attribute

Coworkers that have good relationships at work trust and support one another. They form great teams, and great teams can exceed expectations easier than a group of great individual performers.

Things to consider:

- You Are not obligated to like your coworkers, but you are obligated to treat them professionally and respectfully always, even if it's not reciprocated.

- you might consider a relationship with your

coworkers to be a customer-supplier relationship in some cases. Thinking of them as a customer might bring a different approach to the work you do that influences them.

- Small acts of kindness have a big effect on a co-worker. remembering birthdays, children's names, interests, all contribute to a co-worker thinking of you in a more positive way.

Customers Attribute

depending on your job a customer interaction can be a fun and positive experience, or a very unsettling one. Dealing with customers, one must always remember that you are representing your organization as well as yourself.

Things to consider:

- Good advice that I learned many years ago about dealing with customers was to communicate with them in a way that connects with the emotional state they are in. An angry, dissatisfied customer does not want to hear anyone say, "Let's calm down and talk about this rationally". What must be done first is openly recognize and validate the state of mind they are in. A good response may be "I see that you're quite upset and disappointed. Please explain to me what the problem is." In my experience, it's somewhat surprising how quickly a customer will calm down. Once they do you can start discussing rationally what can and can't be done.
- In the event you are being insulted or bullied by a customer this is something that needs to be addressed with management. No em-

ployee should be subjected to inappropriate treatment by a customer, and you should not have to deal with this yourself.
- Frustration with customer interactions may warrant analysis of the workflow. There may be procedures, signs, general communication, etc. that can be implemented to reduce stress and frustration.

Suppliers Attribute

Suppliers are similar to customers in the sense that when you deal with them you are presenting your company as well as yourself. The advantage of course in that since you are the customer, you have more leverage in the interactions.

Things to consider:
- You are obligated to act professionally and treat them with respect, independent of their behaviour. No employee should be subjected to inappropriate treatment by a supplier, and you should not have to deal with this yourself.
- Frustration with supplier interactions may warrant analysis of the workflow. There may be procedures, signs, general communication, etc. that can be implemented to reduce stress and frustration.

Organization Attribute

This is a very general description of the relationship you have with your company and the broader organization that extends beyond your managers. It may include your manager's manager, your human resource department, and other departments that influence how you do your work.

Things to consider:

- This attribute warrants careful thought and analysis to identify specifically the main issues causing dissatisfaction.
- Frustration can be contagious. If there are a few organization issues bothering you, others than might be insignificant can raise to a "straw that breaks the camel's back" level. Identify the problems and rank them to be addressed. Once one or two are dealt with some lesser ones might even vanish.

Nature Cornerstone - Definition

The nature of your job is what you do at work - the tasks you perform, the skills you develop, use, and exhibit, the responsibilities you hold.
This is the contributor to the Maslow need of Self-Actualization.

Attributes
Assignments/Tasks
These are the activities you do at your job. It can be equipment operation, cleaning, office tasks, sales, project management, etc.
Responsibilities
This is the level of authority and responsibility you have at work. You may be responsible just for your tasks, or you could be a manager, or have responsibility for a business segment (like inventory).
Development Opportunities
This refers to what your organization offers you in terms of training and skills development, and ability to be promoted to higher responsibilities and compensation.
Support for Initiative
This is how your organization responds to your suggestions related to improving your organization's efficiency, productivity, profitability - anything that reflects your interest in going above and beyond to improve things where you work.
Organization Competence
This refers to how proud you are of the organization that employs you. This includes how good your organization is at doing what it's set up to do, how you feel about what it does, and how it goes about its activities (ethics).

General
As children most of us have lofty dreams of what we want to do with our lives. They may be grand plans, like becoming an actor, doctor, or professional athlete. This commonly gives way to

practical outcomes. It's important to look at any work, however, as noble. Your job may not be as flashy as originally hoped, but it contributes to your life, and life possibilities. It takes a bit of life experience to appreciate this, and that self-actualization can be gained with more than just your job.

Dissatisfaction with the nature of your work might seem the most daunting of problems to fix, and that might be so. Or maybe it can be entirely how you've approached your current circumstances. With initiative you might find a lot more room for fulfilment than you originally thought, and that may come from developing the perspective that you have more than you thought you had.

Assignments/Tasks Attribute
This can be simply about boredom at work, or the interest in building skills and advancement for career development. If it's about the latter, it's good to approach this as part of a larger plan.

Things to consider:
- Consider thinking about the tasks you would like to be assigned not solely from the perspective of what you'd *like* to do, but what *you'd like to do* + *what benefits the organization*. Alignment with your organization will create more cooperation for your specific task interests.
- Consider what self-training might do to qualify you for more interesting tasks. Taking online courses is a great way to show initiative that might be encouraged by your organization.
- If your assignments/tasks are creating too much stress and aggravation be sure you have specific suggestions in mind before you raise

this with your manager.

Responsibilities Attribute

Adding responsibilities in your job is of course an excellent way to develop your skill set and increase your compensation. Importantly, more responsibilities usually mean more leadership and more work stress. Some people pursue more responsibilities not realizing that it may improve career prospects in income but reduce satisfaction.

> *Things to consider:*
> - If you seek new responsibilities, recognize that stepping back from them if they are too much may affect your credibility for future requests of this sort. Better to suggest something modest to start than take on more than you can cope with.
> - If you feel your responsibilities exceed your compensation and want them reduced, consider positioning this in a way that benefits your organization rather than a complaint. For example, you can suggest they be re-allocated to a co-worker looking for career development.

Development Opportunities Attribute

In good organizations, career development opportunities are offered to individuals identified as important employees with high potential. Not being offered them might also be the result of a manager not skilled in or thinking about employee development, or just an underestimate of your capabilities. Being asked to be considered for these opportunities is a pleasant circumstance for a manager - it shows that your employee has initiative. It is, however, tied tightly to your perceived work performance.

It's awkward to tell an employee showing initiative that "...they need to focus on doing a good job on what they are currently assigned first." This notwithstanding, new opportunities can possibly take an employee underperforming due to boredom and re-energize them.

Things to consider:

- When seeking new opportunities include how and work you would need to offload can be properly and positively re-allocated.
- Don't wait for tasks to be offered. Think them up and suggest them but be sure that they are tied very closely to group and organization objectives.

Support for Initiative Attribute

It can be incredibly de-motivating to enthusiastically pose some suggestions at work just to get cold weather splashed on them. A good organization will always meet these with positivity, even if they deem it to be ideas then can't, or do not want to, pursue. Sometimes suggestions need persistence, or adjustment, to breakthrough lethargic response from your manager/organization. Maintain positivity and listen carefully to what the feedback is to identify the roadblock.

Things to consider:

- You can float a suggestion informally to sense the response.
- Be prepared to do adequate homework and preparation for suggestions you pose. It's actually a bit annoying for a manager to get suggestions dropped in their lap with the expectation the manager will figure out the details.

Organization Competence Attribute

One example of this attribute that would constitute dissatisfaction is working for an organization that is a weak player in an industry that you seek to develop industry-leading skills in. The other is a very good organization that develops employees well but has an image that you feel self-conscious about (like working for McDonalds).

Things to consider:

- Some consider that it is better to have a job where things are not going well than one in a highly functioning organization - potentially lots of opportunity for experience contributing to improvement in the first case!
- In a poorly functioning organization one can look outside the organization for development - course and industry associations.
- Consider offering to be involved in organizational improvement projects.

CHAPTER 9: SUMMARY

"Folks are usually about as happy as they make their minds up to be."
Abraham Lincoln

This section will be a brief review of the book content to present it in a condensed format. This is to reinforce understanding of the flow of the book, and the key messages. After that, step-by-step instructions are presented for you to use as a guide for driving your *Job Satisfaction Improvement* initiative.

Theory

We started our journey by looking at real-world survey data on job satisfaction, which showed a dismal state of affairs for the overall job satisfaction of working people in the world.

From there we reviewed the conventional definitions of employment *Satisfaction* and *Engagement*. We saw how good companies and organizations recognized the benefits of satisfied and engaged employees, and what steps they take to try to improve this in their organizations.

The benefits of a personal effort to drive one's own job satisfaction was then presented, instead of leaving this to your organization, or happenstance.

A simple goal statement of Satisfaction was crafted to use in this endeavor:

Satisfaction is the fulfillment of those things that we deem are essential, those things that we believe strongly that we deserve, and those things that we desire or hope for.

This led to investigating more deeply the psychology of our drive for satisfaction. The investigation provided the understanding of the mechanics and composition of our motivations and enabled the formation of the basis for interpreting our Job Attributes in terms of these motivations.

Finally, we arrived at a model of job satisfaction - ***The Four Corners Framework*** - providing us a means to organize, value and measure the aspects of our job that contribute to our Job Satisfaction. With this self-awareness in hand, the Transition Plans that provide the clear direction to our personal Job Satisfaction Improvement could be crafted.

Process

Here is the Four Corners Framework Step-by-Step Process:

1. Fill out the Job Satisfaction Self-Assessment form. Take your time understanding each of the twenty Job Attributes. Then assess how you value each (as a Need, Expectation, or Wish), and how you rate each (as Unsatisfied, Satisfied, or Very Satisfied). Use the Good States and Bad States descriptions as guidance for your ratings.
2. Summarize the Self-Assessment by filling in the Four Corners Model template. Take time to absorb the information in both the Assessment and the Four Corners Model. Make any important notes on your thoughts in the Model template form.
3. Fill out the Transition Plans for the attributes

that are valued Needs, then the ones valued Expectations, and finally those valued Wishes in this order. Provide clear and succinct descriptions of Bad States, Good States, and Best States to create crisp insight into where these attributes are now, and where you'd like them to be.

4. To begin the process of closing the Bad-State - Good state gaps you must first honestly assess the state of your Influence factors - *Job Performance* and *Attitude*. As a minimum you must clearly understand how you are perceived on these before proceeding, and how to incorporate your level of influence into the Job Satisfaction improvement process.

5. Begin the Communication Process:
   a. Present your manager with a request for an initial discussion
   b. Have the discussion
   c. Mutually complete actions coming from the discussion (this is the Transition Plan gap closure actions)
   d. Conclusion of process - summary and thanks

Keep in mind that this process is taking you through a "snapshot" analysis of your job and work environment. It very likely will change over time - as your circumstances change, as your work and work environment change, as YOU grow and mature. It is a good idea to update your Four Corners job satisfaction model annually, especially as preparation for an annual performance review, if you have one at your place of employment. Having an updated model will also be of excellent assistance when you are looking for a new job, if you end up in that circumstance. It will help you evaluate how well an opportunity fits with your priorities and will also be a great asset in interviews when questions come about your likes and dislikes, and how you address them.

I leave you with the best of wishes for successful and satisfying work experience, and one final inspirational quote:

"The possibilities are numerous once we decide to act and not react."
George Bernard Shaw

AFTERWORD

This book is also offered in a self-paced video course format at:

https://www.udemy.com/course/job-satisfaction-improvement/?referralCode=F1E6A119FFF4EFE4E9A3

Another self-paced video course offered by the author is *Product Cost - How to Reduce Manufacturing Costs* at:

https://www.udemy.com/course/how-to-reduce-the-cost-of-your-product/?referralCode=6D79199DBB417BBB2750

www.ingramcontent.com/pod-product-compliance
Lightning Source LLC
Chambersburg PA
CBHW070613220526
45467CB00003B/1416